David)

A strong foundation
guides us through
the storm

*Jason Dean* (signature)

**8 Days**
**Till Sunrise**

# 8 DAYS TILL SUNRISE

A True Story of Survival, Rebirth and
Discovering My Purpose in Life

## Jason Dennen

**Manufactured in the United States of America**

ISBN: 979-8-9861473-7-6
Library of Congress Control Number: 2022918211

Follow Jason Dennen

**Social Media Outlets:**

Facebook: facebook.com/jason.dennen.5
Instagram: @ JWDboulder
Email: JasonDennentheHealer@gmail.com

# CONTENTS

# Why?

This book is for all the people who are currently battling through a trial in their lives, for all the people who have lived through a trial and are preparing to live through their next one and for those people who haven't lived through a trial in their lives yet but will as it is only a matter of time before everyone goes through a trial. Living through a trial tests a person and raises questions that they never thought to ask before. It brings self-doubt. *Am I strong enough to overcome this trial? Do I have what it takes?*

Often, we give credit to others for being strong but do not give credit to ourselves because we believe those other people have something we don't have. We need to give ourselves credit for being strong and understand that we have the strength to get through anything in life. The trials we live through help to define who we are.

Everything that I have learned in my life allowed me to survive my trial. Hope is a vital part of getting through these tough challenges we all face. If nothing else, I want this book to bring hope to those who are struggling and to offer assurance that you can also get through a difficult time; you are strong. Part of my responsibility, after surviving my trial, is to share what I have learned with others.

If you read this book and find it helpful, please pass it on to someone else and allow it to help others. We all go through trying times and each of us need a reminder that we are not alone in our struggle. If you read this book and would like me to speak, in person, to a group that you belong to and share my story and message, please contact me at JasonDennentheHealer@gmail.com.

# Acknowledgements

I would like to thank the following people; I would not be here today without their help.

I thank God for watching over me, saving me and giving me purpose again. Thanks to my parents who stayed with me the entire time I was in the hospital and came back to help me with additional surgeries. They took care of so many things I was aware of and so many more things I was not aware of. They took charge of my care and they took on so much and shielded me from so many of the stresses of dealing with my ongoing care and the insurance company. They took care of many things so all I had to do was deal with healing. Thank you to my sister, Melissa, for staying with me in the hospital and feeding me breakfast when I couldn't use my arms to feed myself. Thank you for reminding me that God had a plan for me. Thank you to my brother Greg, who came to the hospital after I got hurt and told me to never accept the doctor's predictions as to how quickly I would heal; thank you for visiting me during the recovery process. Sometimes the older brother needs to try to impress his younger brother by hiking on steep icy trails that I shouldn't have been hiking two weeks after surgery when you came to visit. Thank you to my brother Stu for visiting me in the hospital.

Thank you to my extended family who prayed for me and helped with supporting my parents during my stay in the hospital. Thank you, Lori, for being my emergency contact and having the guts to be the first person to show up at the hospital after the crash and for being willing to tell my parents the full extent of my injuries. Tammy, thank you for being the second person to show up at the hospital the day after the lifesaving surgery and for being the first, and only, person to get kicked out of the ICU. Thank you to all my friends who visited me in the hospital, helped my parents with anything they needed while they lived in Colorado for three and a half months, kept me sane and helped me through my time in the hospital. Thank you to all my skydiving friends who organized a carnival and raised money for me.

Thank you, to all the people who prayed for me and who sent me get well cards.

Thank you to Longmont United Hospital, St. Anthony's Hospital in Lakewood, Vibra Hospital, Spaulding Rehabilitation Hospital and Panorama Orthopedics. Thank you to all the doctors, nurses, therapists and staff who helped me. I couldn't have done it without you. Thank you to Flight For Life Colorado, Longmont Fire Department, and Mile-Hi Skydiving Center for getting me safely from the scene of the crash to the hospital.

Thank you, Rev. Mary Beth Taylor, for assuring me that my story and message was something I needed to share with others and for helping me get started.

Jason Dennen
July 2022

# CHAPTER 1

# The Crash

**James 1:2-4** *"Consider it pure joy, my brothers, whenever you face trials of many kinds, because you know that the testing of your faith develops perseverance. Perseverance must finish its work so that you may be mature and complete, not lacking anything."*

On a clear June day, the sun crept over the horizon and its rays illuminated the Flatirons. This was the view that I had stared at every morning since moving to Boulder, Colorado. It is a view that makes me happy to be alive and hopeful about the upcoming day. Little did I know it would be the last sunrise that I would see for eight days.

My eyes were glued to the beautiful rock faces of the Flatirons as I drove south of town to one of my favorite running trails to start a much-anticipated Saturday. I ran uphill for 30 minutes, seeing barely a soul on this quiet trail. When I reached the top of the loop, I picked up the pace on a slight downhill that led me back to my car. I finished the trail and stared at the Flatirons on the entire drive back home, as the Flatirons were glowing brighter than normal that day. On a day like this, anything seems possible.

Upon returning home, I ate some breakfast, picked up my gear and headed to the airport for another day of skydiving. I had started skydiving about three and a half years earlier. It had become a weekly event in my life. It was an escape from normal everyday life. When I was at the airport, all that existed was the present moment. It was a refuge from all the other things in my life that I wasn't happy with. It would put me in a child-like state as I was only aware of my immediate surroundings and my smile was never wider than it was when I was at that airport.

I had started skydiving for two reasons. The first reason was that I questioned whether I could do it or not. It was the way a lot of my life's adventures started. I would become aware of an activity through reading about it or seeing it in person and wondering if I was capable of doing it. Whether it was racing triathlons, learning to rock climb, ice climb or quitting my job and moving halfway across the country to Colorado, where I didn't know anyone. There is a big difference between thinking you can do something and taking action; taking on the challenge. I suppose I have a need to test myself and to prove to myself that I am capable of whatever challenge I have my eyes on. Riding my bike past the airport four years earlier allowed me to see parachutes in the sky and I wondered how I would handle jumping out of a plane, deploying a parachute and guiding it safely to earth.

The second reason was that I was going through a difficult time in my life. I felt like I was moving through life in quiet desperation. About two years before I started skydiving, I had accepted a new role at work; a promotion that I worked so hard to finally receive. Unfortunately, what no one told me was that it would require 12-14 hours a day for years on end, with no breaks, as every season of the year was busy season. Sure, I had the vacation days to take but there never seemed any time to take them as one overlapping project after another with short, never ending, deadlines sucked me into just getting through each day to survive to the next. I couldn't sleep more than a few hours without waking up to stare at the ceiling, worrying about all the things I had to get done. My chest seemed to be tight all the time from all the stress. The job was killing me, slowly. I was miserable and needed an escape. I had always been an endurance athlete and would normally bike or run long distances for hours each week to get through life's stresses. But because of all the hours I was working, I just couldn't find the energy to consistently run or bike at all in the little free time I had after work. On the weekends, if I wasn't working, I was so tired from the week at work that I tried to catch up on sleep; at least when I slept, I wasn't stressing out about work. I felt stress all my waking hours. I didn't like who I had become. I felt like I had lost my purpose in life; it was a hollow feeling. I had to find something to smile about. The nice thing about skydiving was that I didn't have to train for endless hours to be able to jump out of the plane each week. I could just show up on a Saturday and let gravity take care of everything once I exited the plane.

I had been at the airport a few hours and had jumped two times so far that day. I had just packed my parachute and was ready for my third jump of the day. I checked my gear to make sure all my equipment was in good working order and that all the straps that secured the equipment to me were properly secured to my body. All the skydivers boarded the plane after the plane pulled up in front of us. The plane took off and started climbing to altitude. I started to follow my normal routine. I would check my gear at least twice to make sure it was all still in good working order, and I would say a prayer. I would pray to be watched over and would ask to have the strength and awareness to take care of any emergencies that might occur during the skydive.

A few minutes later, the plane reached the proper altitude. The yellow light was turned on in the back of the plane, which alerts the skydivers to open the door. A moment later, the green light turned on, which signals that the pilot is ready for us to start jumping out of the plane. I checked my gear one more time and then exited the plane. I deployed my parachute at the predetermined altitude, and it deployed and inflated as expected. I started flying my parachute to the landing area. I was setting up for landing on the grassy field that I had landed on hundreds of times previously. My parachute was descending as expected and I was flying into the wind. Flying into the wind when landing is preferred as is slows down the forward speed of your parachute and makes for an easier, softer landing. I was about 150 feet off the ground when, out of nowhere, a huge gust of wind hit me from behind from the opposite direction in which the wind had been gently blowing. The gust of wind picked me up in my harness and shoved me violently forward. My parachute accelerated rapidly. As I looked down, I could see the grass that I wanted to land on was rapidly moving under my feet and I was quickly approaching a fence and a row of airplane hangars (metal buildings that house airplanes). I was unsure of whether I had enough room to land on the grass or whether my increased speed would put me on a collision course with the fence and the building behind it.

I only had about 5 seconds before I would land. I had to determine immediately what action to take. At 150 feet off the ground, I was too low to turn my parachute to avoid the building and fence. Turning a parachute requires the skydiver to pull on a handle which partially collapses the side of the parachute and then the parachute will turn toward the partially collapsed side. Turning the parachute also makes the parachute accelerate toward the ground. A turn at this moment would have likely killed me on impact, or at best injured me severely, as the diving parachute would have crashed into the ground at a high rate of speed, so turning was not an option. My only other option was to do nothing and hope that I had enough room to land on the grass before the fence. I decided the best option was to do nothing. I thought: *Whatever is going to happen, is going happen, at this poin*t.

The seconds started to tick down.

5- I took a deep breath and completely relaxed.

4-I looked at the building and the fence, which were coming at me rapidly

3-I thought there might be a 30 percent chance of landing on the grass

2- I thought there might be a 10 percent chance of landing on the grass

1-I acknowledged I was going to hit the fence and I was going to hit it at a high rate of speed

The fence was a cattle fence; it had three strands of wire, equally spaced, and was held up by some stakes in the ground. I could feel my chest and abdomen hit two of the wire strands and those strands got extremely tight around my body before they quickly snapped as I was moving so quickly, and hit the fence with so much force, that I ripped the fence out of the ground. The airplane hangar stood about ten feet behind the fence so as soon as I broke through the fence, I impacted the building almost immediately, as the fence did nothing to slow me down. I hit the building head-on, going 30 mph.

I had been living through a difficult trial in my life over the past four and a half years and it felt like there was no way out; I was failing to live a life with purpose. Little did I know, the current trial that I was enduring was merely a warm-up for the real trial that had just begun with my impact into the side of the airplane hangar.

The impact left a huge dent in the metal building. I hit the building and fell to the ground. I thought I said out loud immediately after impact, "I'm okay". Months later, I was told that once I hit the building the skydivers that were in the equipment tent, about 100 yards from the airplane hangars, rushed over to me and the first thing I said to them was, "Don't call anyone, I'll be okay just give me a minute." I was blacked out when I said that; I blacked out almost immediately after hitting the hangar. Luckily, none of them listened to what I said as they could see my injuries were severe and they could see I was having trouble breathing. They immediately called 911 and continued to talk to me. I don't remember much from that time period, other than hearing the voice of one of my instructors who had helped train me to skydive a few years prior. I'm not sure what he said, but I will never forget his voice and who he was.

Why would I say, "Don't call anyone, I'll be okay, just give me a minute"? I was blacked out, so I did not consciously say it. It was like my default settings took over. Anytime I had previously gotten hurt, doing anything, I had always gotten up as quickly as possible. I had the mindset that if I could get up and fight through whatever pain I was in, I could overcome whatever was wrong and keep going. If I got up, the injury wasn't bad; I would be okay. In my current condition, there was no way I could get up off the ground under my own power, but my body and mind had started to fight. I didn't have to tell my body and mind to fight or what was needed. My mind and body had been trained to fight and had been put in physically difficult conditions throughout my life. Certainly nothing close to what I was going through at this point, but my body had been practicing survival for years. My body remembered years earlier, when I had been on the verge of succumbing to hypothermia on the side of a mountain in the Teton mountain range of Wyoming. On that mountain, I said to myself, *If I survived the last minute, I can survive the next minute.* After saying that for an hour, I then said, *If I survived the last hour I can survive the next hour.* Once I survived two hours, then I knew I could survive the next two and before I knew it, I had survived the night and the sun rose and the temperature started warming up a little and I was able to descend the mountain and survive. So, when my body and mind sensed that something was horribly wrong, they both started fighting with the life that was still left in my body. I wasn't there mentally to coach my body to do what it needed to do to survive, my body just remembered, from the Tetons, what to do and it went into action; fighting to make my heart pump and my lungs breathe to keep me alive as survival was not guaranteed.

CHAPTER 2

# The Miracle

**Mark 10:27** *"Jesus looked at them and said, 'With man this is impossible, but not with God; all things are possible with God.'"*

The emergency personnel were on scene within four minutes as the Fire Chief just happened to be two miles away at the time of the crash. My equipment was cut off and I was placed on a backboard; my neck was stabilized for the ambulance ride to the nearest hospital, which was, luckily, only a few miles away. At the first hospital, my condition was quickly assessed, and they called for the Flight for Life helicopter because of the dire nature of my injuries. I needed to be transported immediately to a level 1 trauma center to be cared for. A level 1 trauma center is for the most severely injured people with complex injuries. The helicopter rushed me 50 miles to the nearest level 1 trauma center. I briefly must have gained consciousness as I heard the rotor blades of the helicopter at some point during the flight to the hospital.

I was immediately transported from the helicopter into surgery. Immediate surgery was required to save my life. The blunt force trauma my body had been subjected to when I hit the building caused widespread destruction to my body. The most critical injury was to my heart. I hit the left side of my ribcage so hard that ten of the twelve ribs on my left side broke and violently impacted my heart. My heart was forced out of the sac that it normally sits in, called the pericardial sac, and was pushed into the right side of my body and was twisted up. This had to be repaired immediately if I was to survive the day. Survival was still not assured, but the doctor that performed the surgery had hope that the repairs he made would be successful. I was intubated and placed into a coma to protect me from my injuries. The doctors needed to ensure that I wouldn't move or inadvertently cause myself any harm after the surgery.

The day after the emergency surgery, they finally got in contact with my friend Lori, my emergency contact. She was so shaken by the news of my accident that she could not drive herself to the hospital. She had to have her sister drive her and when she arrived, the chaplain met her at the entrance. She thought the worst when she saw the chaplain, but he assured her that I was still alive, but he had to prepare her for what she was about to see. The chaplain brought her up to my room in the ICU. She was updated on my current condition and for the first time, she could see for herself what poor condition I was in.

After seeing me, she had to call my parents to explain the condition that I was in and how serious the situation was. The hospital had contacted my parents earlier that morning but would not fully tell them what was wrong with me over the phone. Lori had to break the news to them and let them know the full extent of how bad I was. My parents started mobilizing on the east coast to fly to Denver to be with me. News spread of the accident and people started praying as there was no guarantee that I would make it through another night.

After calling my parents, Lori came back into my room in the ICU, sat there and watched me. The surgeon that had saved my life the night before entered my room and stood there, staring at me. He stared at me intently for a few minutes. Lori started to feel even more uneasy and concerned than she already was. She asked why he was staring at me and if something was wrong. The surgeon replied that he was staring because he couldn't believe I was alive. He said, "Your friend should have never gotten off that field where he crashed, alive; should have never made it to the first hospital alive; should have never made it to this hospital alive and should have definitely never made it through the surgery alive. No surgeon in this hospital has ever performed this surgery before because no one that had the heart problem that your friend had has ever made it to the hospital alive."

My parents arrived in Denver from the east coast and my friends picked them up and drove them to the hospital to see me. When my Mom and Dad entered my room, my Mom took out her phone and took a picture of my badly broken, motionless, body which was laying in the bed connected to so many tubes and machines and a breathing tube coming out of my mouth. It was not the person she was accustomed to seeing. She later told me she took the picture so that just in case she lost me she would have one last picture.

My Mom then approached my bed and took my hand and said "Jas, it's Mom, I'm here!" and she said I squeezed her hand. It wasn't something that I consciously did, as I have no memory of her voice or her holding my hand, but it gave her hope. She was worried in a way only a parent could be. But no matter how broken my outer shell looked, squeezing her hand showed her I was still in there and I was fighting.

For the first few days post lifesaving surgery, they continued to test the success of the surgery on my heart daily as that needed to be successful to keep me alive. The doctor was unsure enough about the initial success of the surgery that he didn't even close my chest cavity back up after the initial surgery, so that just in case they needed to perform additional emergency surgery, they could access my heart quickly. The nurse explained to Lori that if you lifted my hospital gown the only barrier between my internal organs and the outside world was hospital grade plastic wrap. The nurse asked if she wanted to look at my internal organs, but Lori declined. I think she had already been pressed to her limit just looking at my broken body, laying in that bed, and she was incredibly brave for just showing up at the hospital and having to make that call to my parents.

The doctors were finally satisfied, after performing tests repeatedly, that the initial surgery was successful and that I was going to live. They wired my sternum back together and closed my chest cavity. It was now time to start to repair the rest of my body, which was badly broken.

Over the next few days, I was brought in for multiple surgeries to repair my collapsed lungs, spleen laceration, ruptured diaphragm and my colon had to be pushed back into place. They then fixed my broken left femur, pelvis, which was broken in the front and back, a right wrist fracture and repaired my left elbow, which was dislocated and fractured.

There was nothing they could do to repair my 11 broken ribs and the fracture of my L5 vertebrae, as they just had to heal on their own. The same could be said for my concussion.

CHAPTER 3

# The First Temptations

1ˢᵗ **Corinthians 10:12-13** *"So, if you think you are standing firm, be careful that you don't fall! No temptation has seized you except what is common to man. And God is faithful; he will not let you be tempted beyond what you can bear. But when you are tempted, he will also provide a way out so that you can stand up under it."*

While all the surgeries were occurring, I was waging my own battle. A battle that no one on the outside had any idea was being fought. The coma was filled with darkness, and I was secluded; left to fend for myself. I was tormented by hundreds of nightmares that I could not wake up from. Normally, a person wakes up from a nightmare and can rationalize that the nightmare was just that, a nightmare, and was not real. When you are in a coma, you can't wake up, so those nightmares became my new reality.

The major recurring theme was that I was in bad shape and in need of help and I could not do anything to help myself and no one was going to help me. I value self-reliance and taking care of my own problems and these dreams preyed on my inability to help myself. It is like the nightmares knew my weaknesses and those nightmares exploited them.

The nightmares always started after I had done something terribly wrong. I was never sure what I had done but I could tell from how everyone looked at me, and how they treated me, that they were angry with me for whatever I had done. The first nightmare I remember is that two medical staff carried my broken body into a remote part of the desert and laid me down on the ground and told me they couldn't help me and left.

I may have been in a coma and confused with what was going on, but I did recognize one thing; I was being tempted. Was this nightmare real? Was no one willing to help me? Was I being tempted to give up? Was the bad news I received from the nightmares too much for me to handle? Afterall, no one would know if I just gave up or if the crash was too much for me to handle. I was being indirectly asked if I wanted to live. I had to make that decision without knowing what the consequences were from the crash. What would life be like if I chose to battle through the temptation? I had lost purpose before the crash. Was life worth going back to? Was life worth fighting for and was I willing to deal with all the unknown obstacles that I would encounter if I chose to live? I wasn't ready to give up. It never occurred to me that it was an option. It wasn't in my nature. In my weakened state, I had just enough energy to hold on for now. I ignored the temptation. I gave no reaction to the news that I wasn't going to be helped.

As one nightmare faded into the background, another one started. I was in a waiting room, waiting to see the doctor; I was next to be seen when I heard whispers from the staff that they weren't going to help me, and they were calling the police. In another nightmare, I was broken and laying in someone's backyard while they were trying to enjoy a barbeque and everyone was mad that I was there. This young boy of about 14 looked at me then turned to his Dad and said, "Why don't they just let him die?" That nightmare was a turning point. Up until then, the nightmares tempted me to give up but now, suddenly, they started to become much more aggressive. It was like the initial nightmares were just a warmup for what was about to come. If the initial temptation to have me give up was not working, how far could I be tempted before I would give up? The nightmares may have been becoming more aggressive, but it was also a turning point for me as I had not reacted to the nightmares up until then while in my weakened state. I had just enough energy to hold on; but what that boy said to his father was unacceptable. I was angered for the first time. Telling me I wasn't going to be helped was one thing but what that boy said was so cold and callous. The worst part was that it was coming from a young boy; someone who shouldn't have a mean, hateful bone in his body yet. I would be docile no more. I had just been surviving in this coma long enough; just until I could regain some strength. Now I was ready to fight back!

I realized the only way to overcome the temptation was to confront it. Just like the eagle flies directly into a storm and uses the turbulent wind to soar above the storm to reach clear skies, I had to confront the temptation head on and use the temptation just as the eagle uses turbulent air; to soar above the temptation and find my way out of the storm. Each time I overcame another bout of temptation I soared a little higher. I couldn't see the light through the storm of temptation, but I knew that the light existed beyond the storm and the way to get to the clear sky was to continue to overcome temptation.

Yet another nightmare came. My broken body was lifted by two train conductors and placed into an open-air train car by myself, on a seat facing outward. It was one of those trains you see in Colorado that brings tourists in the summer between two beautiful mountain towns so people can see the amazing landscapes by railway. I was told anyone had the right to shoot me while I was on the train with no repercussions. The train rolled out and as we were chugging along, all fear of being shot left my body. I peacocked my neck and head and yelled, "If you are going to kill me, you better do it now because if you don't do it now, you won't be able to kill me later because I'm coming back from this and I'm coming back strong from this!"

CHAPTER 4

# Sunrise

**Revelation 21:7** *"He who overcomes will inherit all this, and I will be his God and they will be my son."*

The nightmare ended and I opened my eyes for the first time in eight days. I had woken up from the coma just in time to see my first sunrise in eight days. The beams of light were shining in through my hospital room window. I could only open my eyes halfway as my pupils were not ready for a light that was that bright. I had experienced nothing but darkness for the last eight days. When I opened my eyes, besides seeing those rays of sun shining through my window, I was immediately startled by a figure in a white coat leaning over my bed and looking down at me. He said, "You are lucky to be alive." I responded, "Thanks for helping me." I then slowly reached my right arm up to him with an open hand and initiated a high five. I'm not sure the doctor was quite ready for a high five. I can't imagine he is greeted very often by a patient coming out of a coma with a high five. I was excited to be out of the coma. It seemed like I had been battling through that storm for so long in search of light on the other side of all that temptation that wanted to entice me to give up. The high five was a thank you to the doctor, but it was just as much a congratulations to myself. I had gotten through my first trial and I was still here. Facing trials tests your faith and develops perseverance and I knew I would need to continue to build that perseverance for my upcoming journey.

The doctor left the room and I immediately became curious about my current surroundings. I was a bit confused with my current situation. My nurse came in and told me not to try to move. That was not going to be a problem, as I had no desire to move and no idea even if I could. I knew exactly what happened when I crashed into the airplane hangar and what led up to the crash, but I had no idea what was actually wrong with me as I blacked out shortly after impact. I looked down and saw bandages everywhere, and more tubes than I could count, draining blood from various parts of my body. I was surrounded by machines, each one of them making their own unique beeping noise, and there were five or six stands holding IV bags that were attached to me.

I knew I wasn't quite thinking clearly. I assumed, or maybe just hoped, that it was heavy medication that was preventing me from thinking clearly. I hated that loopy feeling and hoped that clear thought would return soon. I was scared to ask if I was paralyzed or not as I knew my parents were in the room and I didn't want to upset them and maybe I was a little scared to ask. In my loopy state, I tried to wiggle my toes. I knew I could at least move my arm from the high five, but I wondered if my legs worked because I couldn't feel them. I started wiggling my toes a bit and I decided to self-diagnose that I was not paralyzed. I didn't say anything to anyone after wiggling them. I thought I would just keep that to myself.

The nurse reappeared and told me that I needed to drink because I hadn't had anything to drink in 8 days and I needed to hydrate myself. My Dad put the straw in my mouth and I drank; then I asked what I was drinking, because it was the best thing I had ever had to drink. Finally, I had gotten him to chuckle. He replied, "You are drinking water." That was the best water I had ever had the privilege of drinking. Who knew city water could be so delicious? I always thought the water I had consumed from mountain streams was the best tasting water I had ever had. At the moment I drank the water, I had instant déjà vu. I couldn't figure out why the experience felt so familiar. Somehow, I was comforted by the feeling of familiarity as everything else in the hospital felt unfamiliar to me. Months later, I realized the feeling came from when I climbed Longs Peak by myself when I first moved to Colorado many years earlier. I had to survive a stormy night without a sleeping bag or tent at over 13,000 ft in winter in below zero temperatures through 12 hours of darkness. I had to move my fingers and toes every few seconds or I would lose feeling in them. After surviving the night and walking my way back to my car, I drove to the first restaurant and food I could get my hands on. That first taste of food tasted as good as that first sip of water did in the hospital. Maybe I was in an unfamiliar place, but I had confronted unfamiliar places before. Maybe surviving that night on the mountain wasn't that different from surviving what I had just been through.

I also learned that night on Longs Peak, what climbing was really about. It had nothing to do with summiting the mountain; that was just a point on the mountain where you could climb no higher and turned around to descend. Climbing was really about all the ups and down and difficulties that you encounter on the way. Opening my eyes from the coma seemed like a high point, or a summit, but summits are fleeting; they last for but a short period of time. Most of my time will be spent ascending and descending from the summit and I would need to spend a lot of time struggling in those valleys; ascending, before I was to stand on top of one of those highpoints again.

After taking a few sips of the best water I had ever consumed, my Dad said, "This is going to be just like training for one of your races." At that moment, without asking what my injuries were, it occurred to me that whatever was wrong with me was fixable. Over the following days, my family started describing all of my injuries to me. The first thing they told me was that there was no brain damage or permanent spinal injuries, which was a relief. I was amazingly lucky. The list of injuries was long and in my hazy state I would forget some of the injuries and ask about specific body parts and what was wrong with them.

The injuries I never had to ask about were my ribs and sternum as those were incredibly painful. I would have to be moved in my bed a few times a day for various reasons. They would roll me to my side and then back. The hospital staff would apologize; you could see the looks on their faces as they prepared to move me as they knew the pain they were about to inflict on me just by rolling me. The pain was almost unbearable and I would sweat profusely. I was usually on the verge of passing out, or at least I wished I would pass out.

I alternated between being completely alert and being in some sort of haze throughout the day and hallucinating due to the lack of sleep and the medications that were in my system. I never seemed to be able to sleep for very long as there was always an alarm going off from one of the machines hooked up to me or a nurse waking me up to check on me. When I was hazy, I had a limited grip on reality and I had to constantly ask when I was finally alert again whether an event that I thought had occurred was real or whether I had dreamed the event happened. The nightmares that occurred during my coma kept recurring in the short periods of time when I could actually fall asleep, which was more like passing out from exhaustion rather than sleeping. The only difference was that now, I could wake up from the nightmares and when I woke up, I would wake up in a full-on panic attack with my heart racing at over 200 beats per minute. My heart felt like it was going to explode out of my chest. I had never had a panic attack before, so I had no idea what was going on. I thought it was something I had to deal with due to my heart surgery. The only thing I could think to do was take the one arm I had that I could move and rub the top of my head with my hand that was in a cast and quietly tell myself to calm down until it would finally go away.

When my haze did lift and I was coherent, I defaulted to a habit I had developed years before; I prayed. I prayed for the strength to make it through the night and to make it through the next day. I was in such pain that I didn't take a single day for granted, I lived them one at a time as it took all my strength just to get to the next.

As the days passed, the nurses would come into the room and remove the drains out of my body, one by one, or one of the IVs would be completed and they would not replace it with another one. One day, they even removed my hook up to one of the machines. This all seemed like progress. I never asked, I just assumed I was making progress until one day they decided to take me out of the ICU and put me into a regular room.

CHAPTER 5

# God's Plan

**Jeremiah 29:11** *'For I know the plans I have for you,' declares the Lord, 'plans to prosper you and not to harm you, plans to give you hope and a future.'*

My sister flew across the country to spend time with me in the hospital. One day, she was sitting in the chair next to my bed and she said, "You know, there is a reason you lived through this accident." I never questioned why the accident had occurred. If that same wind gust had hit me while I was 1000 feet or even 400 feet off the ground, I would have had enough time and enough of a safety margin to turn the parachute away from the building and I would have landed safely. But when it hit me 150 feet off the ground, I had no time, or safety margin, to turn without killing myself in the process. What a difference a few seconds and a few hundred feet make. I never thought that this mattered but my sister was right; there was a reason all this happened. I knew God had a plan for me and this was part of his plan. I was lucky that I didn't know this was the plan before I did that third jump of the day, or I would have gone home early and avoided the crash. I believed that I jumped that third time because this was the plan God had for me; I was lucky because he was watching over me and he picked me to live through the crash. What was I going to do with this second chance at life?

I interpreted the crash as a wakeup call. For the last few years, I felt like I was handcuffed to a treadmill that was forcing me to run at top speed without any break. The new job I took a few years earlier was one of the reasons I was skydiving as an escape. It forced me to constantly work at a feverish pace for an inordinate number of hours. I got so sucked into just getting through the day to survive to another, that I was all consumed with getting the next projects done while five were already in progress. Everything at work was some sort of emergency, all the time. When I finally lifted my head up every few months, I would realize I hadn't done anything but work. I was doing nothing for myself, or anyone else, that was meaningful. I wasn't visiting my family or talking to my friends as much as I wanted to, or should have. I was missing family events and not doing things that I wanted to do; like volunteering at a hospital. Volunteering at a hospital had been on my to do list for years. It just sat there on the list untouched. I felt empty. I felt regret. I wasn't able to break the pattern. I felt like I had abandoned my family and friends and was only really present if there was an emergency. I had neglected my relationships, and for what?

God may have been tapping me on the shoulder, trying to show me the error of my ways; but I suppose I never seemed to get the message. Maybe I needed a more forceful delivery of the message. Something that I couldn't ignore. Whaaaaaaaaaack!!! That building was hard to ignore. His message was finally received.

You could say skydiving almost killed me, but it also allowed me to be reborn and step off the treadmill, take a deep breath and think about how I had turned down the wrong path. The accident was a blessing. I got to see what I wasn't happy about in life before it was too late. I still had time to reevaluate life and try to get back on the path I wanted to be on.

No matter how much I had neglected my relationships over the last few years, all my friends and family were there to support me and be with me when I needed them most. My parents and siblings flew out in those early days to be with me. Friends started visiting once they knew I was out of the coma and it was okay to see me. The get-well cards started pouring in from so many people and sometimes from people I didn't know. The prayers continued to pour in, as they had since the news of the accident spread.

I was weary from all the regret of what I had let my life devolve into and who I had become. While lying in bed, in the darkness, I felt that this was the first time that I had been able to take a deep breath and relax in years. I thought how sad that was. Suddenly a weight was lifted off me. Life became simple again. Survival, getting better, rebuilding myself to who I wanted to be and thanking all those people that stuck by my side was all I needed to worry about.

Lying in bed and not being able to move may have seemed like torture for someone as active as I was. I always used my body to relieve my stress; whether it was running, hiking, biking, climbing or jumping out of planes. The blessing of not being able to walk, or move, was that my normal coping mechanisms were taken away from me. I couldn't deal with my problems by running and getting that endorphin high or spending a day jumping out of a plane so I wouldn't have to face the unhappiness my life had become. When you can't do anything other than lay in the bed and not move, every day, for weeks at a time, it forces you to confront what makes you unhappy. I contemplated the ways that I had disappointed myself with where I had allowed life to take me. I had to truly confront my problems without any break or distractions. I had to beat myself up mentally, make myself feel the pain and regret. Changes are never made when you are happy or content with your current situation. I needed to tear myself down and make myself raw and sore. I had to beat myself down mentally until I retreated to a fetal position and could take no more punishment. Only then could I reemerge and build myself back to the person I wanted to be, the person I needed to be, the person whose life was spared by God to come back and be someone He was glad He saved, the person that He brought back to serve Him and glorify His name.

CHAPTER 6

# Despair

**Hebrews 12:7** *"Endure hardship as discipline; God is treating you as sons. For what son is not disciplined by his father?"*

As the weeks passed, the reality of being bed ridden and feeling like I could not do anything to get better set in; my positive outlook on the future started to deteriorate. I was ready to start getting after it and rehabbing. I wanted to do something to get better once I woke up from the coma but that wasn't possible. My body was nowhere close to being ready to do much of anything. I didn't have the strength to open the top of my yogurt at breakfast, I couldn't reach the button on my bed to adjust the incline by myself and when someone was nice enough to bring me a whole box of clementine oranges, all I could do was stare at them and think that peeling those oranges was just one more thing I couldn't do. I had to rely on someone else to do everything for me; I was extremely demoralized. I was humbled by how weak I was when I couldn't break the seal on the screw off top on a bottle of Gatorade and I watched my 71-year-old mother open it without any effort at all. I hated lying there and not being able to do anything for myself. I reluctantly accepted help as I had no choice.

As I got frustrated by my inability to do anything for myself, I thought nonstop about the guilt I felt for putting my friends and family through this accident. I felt guilt as soon as I woke up from the coma but now, I seemed to think about it 24 hours a day. I couldn't imagine what it must have felt like for my parents to receive a call that their son had been in a terrible accident and that they needed to come right away as he may not survive. How must it have felt for my parents to break that news to my siblings? How did my siblings feel when they heard the news? What did it feel like when my friends heard about the crash? I can't imagine. If I had one wish, I wish I could have taken that pain away from them, so they didn't have to feel it. No one ever blamed me for the crash. They said it was okay; they understood that it was an accident. It was a crazy gust of wind, but I was the one who had decided to jump out of the airplane. I was the one who took the risk but now they were paying for the risk that I took.

My physical therapist would come in everyday and try to move my left arm, which was badly broken and dislocated in the crash. I dreaded her visits. I had to take a deep breath when she would walk into my room as I anticipated the pain that was about to surge through my body once she started treating me. She would move my arm barely an inch or two and the pain was so great that I would be on the verge of passing out from it. Doubt started creeping into my mind. How could I recover from all my injuries when the therapist couldn't move my arm more than an inch or two without me being on the verge of losing consciousness? I didn't seem to be making any progress and the pain was unbearable.

The day finally came when I was to be transported back to my orthopedic surgeons' office so all three of the surgeons could take x-rays and assess the progress of the broken bones that they had fixed. The ambulance came to pick me up and transport me via stretcher. I was depressed and overwhelmed from another one of my sessions with the physical therapist. The ambulance driver came into my room and started picking on me. "Do you think it was a good idea to jump out of that plane? When are you going to jump again?" It was the condescending tone of his voice and how he was asking these questions that put me into a rage. Was it necessary for him to come after me? He thought my lack of response to his question as to whether I would jump again was his cue to ask the same question three more times within two minutes. I felt so angry and so helpless. I was not in the mood to take his abuse. I was stuck with this guy for the next few hours, and he was one of two people who would be picking me up and transporting me from my bed to the stretcher and back. In my condition, I was worried that if I wasn't moved in the most delicate way, the bones that were currently mending could be reinjured; not to mention the pain. I kept my mouth shut and stayed quiet for the next five hours I spent with him.

I took the x-rays; I thought it had been a few weeks since the surgeries and that should be enough time to heal my bones. What did I know? It wasn't like I had the opportunity to ask questions when I was in the coma and they were fixing me. My only experience was that when people I knew broke their arms, they had a cast for four or six weeks and they were healed. What I didn't know was that my broken bones were not your run of the mill breaks, they were all quite bad and required plates, screws and rods to hold the bones together. When the doctor read my medical report aloud from the physical therapist stating that I was on the verge of passing out during physical therapy on my elbow, I heard him dictate to his assistant that the message back to the therapist was to push past the vasovagal response. I do not speak Latin, but it was not difficult to decipher the message. He wanted my therapist to keep pushing my arm and the therapist should not stop unless I actually passed out. If I thought the pain was unbearable already, well, it was about to get worse when I got back to the hospital.

I left the office dejected as I didn't seem to be anywhere close to my bones being healed or to being able to get out of bed. It was back to bed for some underdetermined amount of time. I either didn't have the presence of mind to ask how long it was supposed to take to heal or I just didn't really want to know the answer as I might have become even more depressed. Maybe it was better to be delusional and expect to be fully recovered each time I had a doctor's appointment. I was growing impatient. I had never been in a situation where I couldn't do anything to make an injury better by taking action and rehabbing it. I just had to lie there and wait. The ambulance brought me back to the hospital and placed me softly back into my bed. I bid the ambulance driver farewell and hoped that I would never see him again.

The physical therapist came back in and I knew what that meant; more pain. She had the notes from the doctor, and she had her orders on what she needed to do. You could tell she didn't want to do what she was about to do. She knew she would hear me yelp and curse at the pain as it shot throughout my body. She was going to push my arm until I was about to pass out. The pain was hard to deal with as it didn't seem to be leading to any progress in my recovery. She would close my door when she started her treatment; I'm sure anyone in the hallway could hear me yelling just trying to get through the exercises she put me through. Finally, after an hour, it ended and I was left to my depression and trying to figure out what to do when all I could do was lie there.

My Mom came back in my room and I told her how bad the rehab hurt. I'm assuming she already knew that from hearing the nonstop yelling coming from my room. When I stopped complaining she said, "You know, when I walk around this wing of the hospital, I see a lot of DNR (Do Not Resuscitate) signs on patient's doors. You don't have one of those on your door." That went in one ear and out of the other when she said it. I was too busy licking my wounds because of the pain I was in. It took a day or two, but while I was lying quietly at night in my room, I finally understood what she said. Some of those patients were never going to see the outside of a hospital again. Some of those patients had it much worse than I did. I may have been in bad shape, but I could have had it worse than I did. I could be lying in a room with no hope of ever recovering. One day, I was going to get out of the hospital.

My nurse came to my room the next morning and could see I wasn't doing well. She had been in the room when the ambulance driver had been needlessly harassing me. She knew how much that affected me and she told me she could see it in my face. She said, "I know you are feeling down now, and you are feeling like nothing is changing day to day, but I want you to know this is just your condition today. It won't be your condition forever. You will get better, little by little." She then asked if I wanted to see the psychiatrist. I had never been to one before. I thought for a second and said, "Sure, why not?"; it wasn't like I had anything else to do other than lie in bed all day, every day. Any distraction from just lying there was welcome.

The psychiatrist came in the next morning; he sat down and asked me what was bothering me. I told him about all the guilt that was weighing heavily on me and the general feeling of being helpless. After two minutes of listening, he started listing off names of drugs: Prozac, Zoloft, Lexapro and Cymbalta. He asked if I wanted to take some of that medication. I recognized one or two of the drugs from tv commercials as being anti-depressants. I asked what they were for and why would I want to take them. He said, "They will cut out the highs and lows." I immediately became infuriated. I couldn't believe he would come in and listen to me for 2 minutes and this was his solution; to drug me up and take all the pleasure and sadness out of life. At this point, it was mostly sadness and self-loathing, but it was my sadness and I needed to feel that discomfort. I didn't want my feelings and emotions softened or muted to make me feel less, or nothing. I saw the offer for what it was: an offer to take a short cut. He was tempting me to take the easy way. He was taking a short cut himself. If he made me docile, it made his job easier because he wouldn't have to do anything. He would just pass me off to the next hospital and let them deal with it. I didn't take the shortcut when I was tempted in the coma, and I wasn't taking the shortcut now. There was a reason I was lying in the bed with no use of my legs or most of my upper body. It was my time to confront my life, not a time to kick my problems down the road. Those highs and lows were mine and he was not taking those away from me. I looked directly into the psychiatrist's eyes and told him to get out and never come back. I think he must have seen the rage in my eyes. Without a word he quietly got up and left.

I was no longer feeling self-pity or sadness; I was in a full rage. Either he was completely incompetent or a genius. Whatever he was, he entered my room and got kicked out within three minutes.

CHAPTER 7

# Talents

**Matthew 25:14-30** *"Again, it will be like a man going on a journey, who called his servants and entrusted his property to them. To one he gave five talents of money, to another two talents, and to another one talent, each according to his ability. Then he went on his journey. The man who had received the five talents went at once and put his money to work and gained five more. So also, the one with the two talents gained two more. But the man who received the one talent went off, dug a hole in the ground and hid his master's money. After a long time the master of those servants returned and settled accounts with them. The man who had received the five talents brought the other five. 'Master' he said, 'you entrusted me with five talents. See, I have gained five more.' His master replied, Well done, good and faithful servant! You have been faithful with a few things; I will put you in charge of many things. Come and share your master's happiness!' The man with the two talents also came 'Master,' he said you entrusted me with two talents; see, I have gained two more.' His master replied, Well done, good and faithful servant! You have been faithful with a few things; I will put you in charge of many things. Come and share your master's happiness!' Then the man who had received one talent came. 'Master' he said, 'I knew you are a hard man, harvesting where you have not sown and gathering where you have not scattered seed. So, I was afraid and went out and hid your*

33

*talent in the ground. See, here is what belongs to you.' His master replied, 'You wicked, lazy servant! So, you knew that I harvest where I have not sown and gather where I have not scattered seed? Well then, you should put my money on deposit with the bankers, so that when I returned I would have received it back with interest. Take the talent from him and give it to the one who has ten talents. For everyone who has will be given more, and he will have an abundance. Whoever does not have, even what he has will be taken from him. And throw that worthless servant outside, into the darkness, where there will be weeping and gnashing of teeth.'''*

I continued to build my anger for the remainder of the daylight hours. I started to calm down after the sun had set and I was in my room, by myself, in the darkness. The hospital could be chaotic and loud during the day, but few people were around at night. It was quiet except for the beeping of the machines that I was hooked up to. By that time, I couldn't even hear the beeping of the machines anymore. After hearing the beeping 24 hours a day for weeks on end, you just tune the noise out. The quiet nights were a good time to reflect on my life, but they could also be a time for my thoughts to torture me and to bring me down and make me doubt myself and question whether I was ever getting out of the hospital.

That night, I pulled out the iPad that my sister had given me shortly after I got out of the coma. I had watched it a few times previously, but all the shows seemed to be depressing. I suppose watching the ten-part series on the Flint Michigan water crisis wasn't the most uplifting show to watch. Up until that night, the iPad sat mostly unused.

For some reason, I decided to pick it up and I looked through the movies on all the channels my sister had loaded on it. I saw that 'Into the Wild' was an option. It was a movie I had watched in the theater years before which was based on a book that I had previously read multiple times. It is a story about a young man on a journey; a journey to seek adventure and to confront the unknown. The young man really wanted to test himself against the brutal realities that exist in nature. I finished watching the movie and that put me in the mindset to think more about my own situation. That night, I felt the brain fog I had been living with since the accident, because of the medication they had me on, finally lift. I felt mental clarity for the first time since the accident. I realized part of the anger I had felt earlier in the day was anger I felt with how I was dealing with my current reality; feeling sorry for myself and helpless. Was that who I was? Was I really unable to do anything to make progress? Maybe I couldn't move but there must be something I could do to make progress.

I thought of the parable of the talents, Matthew 25:14-30; something I had learned years ago. I realized I was the servant who had buried his talents. I was not using my talents to recover. I had to change my perception. I had to create momentum. I had to make some sort of progress. All I was l doing was fixating on the things I couldn't do. I needed to find things that I could do now and use the talents I currently had; not mourn the ones I didn't have.

I had just confirmed that my mind was finally clear and working properly. I had just avoided being made into a docile zombie by the psychiatrist earlier that day. I could train my mind for the journey ahead. I looked back at the movie and that made me connect to the journey I was embarking on. It made me connect to journeys I had already been on in my life. Any journey will have its ups and downs. I will travel through unknown territory and confront challenges that I had never confronted before. I had to start getting comfortable with being uncomfortable. Comfort was my enemy and accepting that I would be uncomfortable through this journey was the way I would get through it. Comfort was a form of temptation that I had to overcome. Comfort was the easy road, and the easy road was not the way I was going to get out of the hospital. I finally admitted to myself that I was not going to fully recover in a day, a month or even a few months. I needed to just concentrate on getting a fraction of a percent better each day, just like training for a race where I strive to get slightly better each day. Suddenly, I felt a huge weight lift off my shoulders. The unrealistic pressure I had been putting on myself to get completely better all at once, when that wasn't physically possible, had been weighing me down. I was overwhelmed by all the injuries I had. Now, I gave myself the permission to just get slightly better each day. Slightly better each day was going to compound over time and before I knew it, all those small improvements would add up to a huge improvement. Each day going forward, I watched a new movie about another journey; whether it was about a group of four women that rowed across the Pacific Ocean or a gentleman who was paralyzed who decided to push his wheelchair across the entire country. I would seek out documentaries about others who had gone through tough journeys to see how they used their minds to get through those journeys so I could condition my mind for my journey ahead.

Besides training my mind for the journey, I could train myself to deal with pain. I knew that pain would continue to be a part of my journey and was not going to go away anytime soon, if at all. Every few hours, nurses would make their rounds to my room to check on me and try to make me as comfortable as possible. They would always ask for my pain level and would be happy to hand out any pain medication I wanted, or they thought I needed. Sometimes, if I declined, they would go as far as asking me if I was sure I didn't want any pain medication. They would always say someone with my injuries should be taking more pain killers. I don't blame the nurses as they were trying to make sure I was as comfortable as possible, but I had to ask myself anytime they offered pain medication, *Am I taking pain pills for pain or as a crutch?* Taking pain medication to zone out and not deal with my current situation was a temptation and it had to be avoided. I decided that as much as I could endure from that day forward, I would say no to pain pills and learn to manage pain with my mind. I must be able to deal with pain if I was ever going to get to my intended destination. I had to make pain my companion.

Guilt had been weighing on me for weeks. I had to let go of the guilt I was feeling as it was destroying me and doing me no good. No one else blamed me for the crash; I was punishing myself and blaming myself. Spending so much time feeling guilty didn't solve any of the problems I had; it was just wasted energy. The best gift I could give my family and friends was to get out of the hospital, become independent again and get back physically, as close as I could, to my pre-accident self. I had to forgive myself in order to move forward.

I had to start recognizing the gifts that people gave me and learn to utilize them. A gift is useless unless it is utilized and it was my responsibility to figure out how it needed to be used; whether it was the iPad my sister gave me, my Dad telling me my recovery would be like training for a race, my Mother reminding me that my situation could have been much worse or even the psychiatrist, as he unknowingly gave me a gift.

I couldn't give failure a voice. There were going to be difficulties along the way. I needed to trust the process of recovery. I would never get to where I wanted to go by admitting defeat at the beginning of the journey. I would no longer allow myself to question if I could recover. If I continued to allow the same message of doubt to replay in my mind enough times, I might start believing it. I would no longer allow doubt to creep into my mind.

Ever since I had woken up from my coma, hospital personnel would ask me repeatedly what happened when I crashed. I would recount exactly what happened. After telling the story many, many, many times over the first few weeks in the hospital, I was tired of telling the story. I would always tell it if I was asked but I was reliving the accident daily, in my own mind, and then again every time I told the story. I then realized that telling the story was not for my benefit; the reason I had to tell it was to help other people. I realized those people in the hospital saw so many terrible things and so often had to watch sad outcomes. I could see the sadness and the fatigue in their eyes. What if telling this story gave them hope? If I came back from this accident and they saw a positive outcome from someone who should not be alive, maybe they could see how important everything they did for patients each day was and what a huge difference they made in a patient's life. I realized that every time someone new came into my room, they would read my medical report and see all my injuries and not know what to expect. They would start talking to me and I could see they were curious; they would slowly build up the courage to ask about the crash. I could tell they didn't want to upset me, but they really wanted to hear the story. I suppose not everyone comes into the hospital every day and has such a crazy accident and was still alive to tell the tale. I would notice, as I proceeded to tell the story, that they would start to relax a little as I would throw in a few jokes so they knew it was okay to joke around about the crash with me. Their demeanor would change as I told the story. By the end, they would be smiling and whatever frustration or fatigue they came into my room with went away; at least for the time they were in my room. I decided that the story was not a burden to bear, it was a gift to give, and I needed to continue to tell that story.

After that pivotal night, my mental approach to everyday going forward changed. I started looking forward to the physical therapist coming in everyday for those one-hour, unbearable pain sessions. Each night, at 8pm, I would start getting psyched up for the following day's session. The sessions were still incredibly difficult, I just went into the session with a new mindset. For that hour each day, I was yelling as the pain surged in my arm and shoulder. I told the therapist to ignore the yelling and do what she had to do to make me get better. At the end, I would thank the physical therapist for all her work and give her a high five. It was like a little celebration that I had made it through another one of those awful sessions. I would tell her I was looking forward to the next day; she would look at me like I was a little bit off my rocker. I convinced myself this was the way forward to recovery. The elbow and shoulder were the first step. If I could take this pain and build up momentum in my recovery, it would continue to the rest of my body. I had now reassociated the meaning of that unbearable pain. Now pain equaled progress. Pain became a little more bearable when I accepted pain was the price to pay for making progress.

# CHAPTER 8

# Dim No More

**Psalms 18:28** *"You, O Lord, keep my lamp burning; my God turns my darkness into light."*

I started to fall into a daily routine for the first time since I had arrived in the hospital. I created my own regimen for making progress. It made me accountable for doing certain tasks every day to improve my health; it would have been easy to just lie in bed and do nothing. No one was going to tell me to do something if I didn't want to. I had to take advantage of my time to get better and progress. I also decided to have the philosophy of saying yes to anything anyone asked me to do. The people in the hospital were there to help me and I assumed anything they asked me to do was going to be safe and I assumed I should have the ability to do it. I assumed that the more I said yes, the more they would want to help me get better. I would smile when people came into my room and would crack a few jokes. I figured if the hospital personnel enjoyed being in my room, the more likely they were to come back and to give me more things to do so I could get better.

My daily regimen revolved around the hour-long pain sessions for my elbow and shoulder, my other physical therapist would come in daily to wrap my body in a net and pick my body up off the bed with a little crane, aka a Hoyer lift, and put me in a big, padded wheelchair. He would wheel me out of my room just so I could see different scenery other than the inside of my room. He would have me move my legs to try to keep some muscle tone in them. Since I wasn't allowed to put any weight on them until they healed, I had to do something to try to keep the muscles from withering away. I continued my mental training by watching new documentaries each day about someone overcoming challenges. I continued to expand my tolerance for pain by staying away from pain killers.

I really felt like I had started to build momentum. I felt like some of the obstacles I had been encountering seemed to subside. My wound care team came in for their weekly visit to check how all my incisions were healing. They would remove all my bandages, assess the progress and redress all my wounds. My wounds were numerous, so it took them awhile to work on me. I had a 12-inch incision on my left leg, a 12-inch incision on the back of my left arm, a six-inch incision on my right wrist, an eight-inch incision on my pelvis below my waist and the biggest one went from my clavicle to right below my belt line, affectionately known as a zipper. They finished dressing my wounds and they left my room. Moments later, I started to get unbearable pain in my right upper abdomen. Over the previous month I would be woken up by pain in my upper abdomen almost daily, but the pain was no more than a 6 out of ten so it didn't seem like a big deal. I had assumed it was part of the healing process, but this pain was a ten out of ten. I thought it was related to the new bandage because the abdomen pain was a night pain, not a 4:00 in the afternoon pain. I asked them to come back, and I explained the pain. They said my pain had nothing to do with the new bandages, but they redressed it anyway. They were right; the new dressing did nothing to stop the pain. It became increasingly worse. The doctor came in and started trying to figure out what the problem was. He seemed stumped as to why I was feeling so much pain and ordered a blood draw for the following morning to see what they could find out. For the next two days I was writhing in constant pain.

The test results finally came back; the doctors realized that one of the daily medications they had been giving me over the last few weeks had poisoned my liver. For the last two days, my liver had been screaming out to stop the medication as major damage was being done. The doctor explained that they had to give me an antiserum to detox my liver, administered via a three-day IV drip. They hooked the IV drip up and the pain seemed to go back down to a six out of ten. About an hour later, both of my physical therapists came into my room; they sat me up for the first time since the accident. My legs were free to hang off the side of the bed. It felt great; I was making progress. Sure, they had to hold me up as I was so weak I couldn't hold myself up; but being in the seated position was better than lying down. A minute or two passed and I started sweating profusely. I was sweating through my gown from just sitting there. I started seeing spots and feeling dizzy. I felt like I was about to pass out. I had to ask the therapists for a break as I told them I needed a minute as I felt terrible. They laid me back down and left the room to give me a break. I started to feel discouraged for a moment. I wondered how I was ever going to walk if I couldn't even sit up for more than a minute without feeling the way I did. Within two minutes, I knew something was wrong. A nurse came in to check on me and realized something was going terribly wrong. It turned out I was allergic to the medication they were using to detox my liver and I was going into anaphylactic shock. Six nurses and the doctor sprinted in and started working on me and chaos ensued. I looked at the doctor and said, "Am I supposed to stay awake for this or am I going to die if I go to sleep?" He didn't answer, and then the lights went out. They must have put me out as they were sticking all kinds of needles into my arms. I woke up in a different room hours later. I guess the answer was that I wasn't dying, but it would have been nice if the doctor had answered me; after all, I asked calmly and politely.

When I woke up, my parents told me the reason why I had passed out and I started reassessing the doubts I had had when I couldn't sit up earlier that day. I looked at this setback as part of the journey. Whenever I had a setback, I had to remind myself where I have come from already, where I am now and where I am headed. It wasn't that long ago that I was lying on the ground next to that airplane hangar fighting for my life; not that long ago that I was fighting temptation in that coma and not that long since I was feeling helpless. Where was I now? Well at least I sat up today for a minute, I had a positive mindset, and I was making some progress toward my recovery. Where was I going? I was working toward recovery. I was working toward eventually getting out of the hospital.

The doctors forced me to rest for a few days, as they didn't want to tax my body further after my recent incident. They continued to give me the antiserum at a slower rate and after three or four days I was finished. The liver pain started to slowly dissipate; down to a one or two out of ten. I couldn't wait to start therapy again as lying in bed all day, without having the distractions of physical therapy, was starting to get old and monotonous. Therapy may have been horribly painful, but it made me feel like I was working on my recovery rather than doing nothing.

Therapy resumed and my shoulder finally felt like it had a little bit more range of motion than it had before. The progress may have been small or unnoticeable to anyone else, but I held onto that small improvement as a sign of the small improvement I was striving to make each day. I started to do additional therapy on my own. I started using my right arm to force my left arm to move more than it could on its own. I would press to the point of pain and would hold it there and long as I could. I would repeat it for hours at a time. I would move my feet around under my blankets trying to maintain my ankle mobility and keep my calf muscles from withering away.

After another week or two of building momentum, one of the doctors, during one of his routine checks, started to get concerned that my lungs were on the verge of collapsing again. More machines were brought into my room and attached to me once again. One of the ways I had gauged progress was by being disconnected from the machines that were monitoring me. Connecting me to more of them was a step back, at least in my mind. They hooked me up to oxygen for the first time since waking up from the coma. They hooked the blood pressure cuff on my arm which started pumping up every hour 24 hours a day and woke me up every time it started pumping up. They also hooked up a pulse monitor on my finger which glowed a bright green light. Late one night, as I could not sleep because of all the machines and their nonstop noise, I was lying there, by myself, at 3:00 AM and I stared at my glowing finger which was illuminating the dark room. I was frustrated and couldn't stop staring at that light. I could hide the light under my sheet or blanket and it still shined through. Why was it so bright? I realized that light symbolized the light I wanted to emit out into the world. My light had been dimmed for the last few years and I couldn't figure out how to make it bright again. Was this trial I was living through a catalyst to make my light bright again? I had to be more like that light. The blankets I put over that light were a metaphor for all those things I had been going through in life that had been dimming my light. Just the way the light was glowing through that blanket, I had to figure out a way to make my light shine no matter what challenges I was going through in life. I started to sing 'This Little Light of Mine'…

> This little light of mine
> I'm going to let it shine
> Oh, this little light of mine
> I'm going to let it shine
>
> This little light of mine
> I'm going to let it shine
> Let it shine, all the time, let it shine

I must have been tired and delirious as I never sing out loud. It is an old song that I had I learned as a child in Sunday school. I kept singing it until I passed out; exhausted from the sleep deprivation caused by the constant noise of the machines and that green light that would never be dimmed.

They ran more tests in the hospital and then sent me to another hospital for additional testing. I never believed my lungs were collapsing and I started to get annoyed because I had to stop therapy for a few days while they figured out their plan of action. Ultimately, they decided they would take a wait and see approach and let my body try to heal the partial collapse on its own. Another small setback, but it just added to my focus toward getting better. The momentum I had started building was too much for this little setback to slow me down.

CHAPTER 9

# My Old Friend

**Ephesians 4:32** *"Be kind and compassionate to one another, forgiving each other, just as in Christ God forgave you."*

It was finally time to go back for more x-rays so my orthopedic doctors could check the progress of my bones healing. My ambulance driver arrived. What were the chances that it was the same ambulance driver that thought asking me obnoxious questions a few weeks earlier was the way to treat a patient? As soon as he walked in, I knew I had two options: I could either hold our first encounter against him and not interact with him, or I could give this guy a second chance. Maybe he had been having a bad day the first time he met me, and he happened to take his bad mood out on me. I certainly hadn't been having a good day when I met him weeks earlier and he certainly hadn't helped. As a patient in a hospital, it was easy to get caught up in believing that I was the center of the universe. Whenever someone came into my room, all questions revolved around my wellbeing; "How are you feeling? What do you want to eat? How is your pain level?" What I had to take into account, was that all the people helping me have lives outside of the hospital; outside of helping me. They knew everything going on in my life as I was stuck there 24 hours a day, but they had their own problems and life issues to deal with that I was not aware of. *So, I thought, let me start asking him questions and see how his day was going and what he likes to do.* After the 45-minute ambulance ride to the doctor's office we started to warm up to each other. We may have not started off well the last time we were together but this time we were having a few laughs and we were talking about life outside of his job as an ambulance driver and my life outside the hospital. During the previous visit to get x-rays, I had been forced to lie on the ambulance stretcher for four hours as the multiple doctors took forever to see me. An ambulance stretcher is not meant for comfort as my shoulders were wider than the side bars that were supposed to keep me from falling off the edge and those bars dug into my back for those four hours in the office and the hour and a half round trip to and from the doctor's office. This time, the ambulance driver wouldn't allow the same thing to happen again. He became my advocate. Every few minutes, he would walk up to the front desk and continually ask when the doctors were going to see me; he reminded them of my condition and that I couldn't lie there for a long period of time because of the pain. I didn't prompt him to do this or even complain to him that I was uncomfortable. He just took it upon himself to look out for me. The multiple appointments this time took only two hours, instead of four. I was so grateful that he was looking out for me. We spent the ride back to the hospital laughing and telling stories. I certainly learned a lesson that day. I needed to be more aware of what other people were going through in life and how that could affect their mood. I needed to consider that maybe there was a reason they were acting a certain way. Maybe taking a second to consider what someone else was going through, before I reacted, could turn a bad situation into a positive situation for everyone involved.

The ride home from the doctors' visit was also uplifting as the x-rays showed that they could take the casts off my right wrist and forearm and off my left arm, which had been covered from my shoulder all the way to my wrist. They gave me temporary casts and said I could wear them if I wanted to or needed to wear them. I took them back to the hospital with me, but I never put them on again.

The doctors also x-rayed my pelvis and broken leg. They said that the bones weren't healed enough to put any weight on my legs yet. I was going to have to go back to lying in the bed again. I had been hoping that my legs and pelvis were healed but I was thankful that the casts had been removed from my arms. I decided that instead of mourning the fact that I couldn't put weight on my legs I would celebrate that I could use my arms more than I could previously as my range of motion was greater without the casts on. I realized that this gave me a month to concentrate on the rehabilitation of my arms as it would be another month before I could have my legs x-rayed again. When I got back to the hospital, I discovered that without the casts I could reach the button on my bed that allowed me to adjust the angle of my bed. It seems like such a little thing, but you can't imagine how dependent it made me on other people when I couldn't do it myself. I couldn't tell you how many times I wanted to adjust my bed and I just left it how it was because I was sick of bothering people to perform such a little task. It was just one more little thing that kept the momentum going. It was a little thing, but it was a visible sign of progress. I would move my bed up and down all day, even when I had no desire to move it. It was a little piece of my independence that I had just gotten back.

The next morning, I woke up for breakfast and they brought in my usual breakfast of yogurt and cereal. I decided I was going to try to open the top of the yogurt myself. Up until then, I had been so weak that I couldn't open the container myself. On my second try I was able to open it; another sign of progress. I was getting excited.

A few days later, the wound care team came back for their weekly follow up and they removed all my bandages; they let me know that my incisions were healed enough that they didn't have to put the bandages on again. Later that day was the first time I had been able to have a shower in nine weeks. I felt more like a dog going to the groomer for a cleaning as I had to lie on a gurney as I was sprayed down with a hose, but I hadn't felt this clean in a long time. Up until then, because of my incisions, I couldn't get wet so I could only get cleaned by wet wipes, which don't make you feel clean. My hair felt like a giant ball of matted grease. Feeling clean for the first time in so long felt great.

After the insurance company heard that the casts on my arms came off, they were already pushing me to move to the next hospital which would be the rehabilitation hospital. The insurance company was always looking to save money and transfer me to the next hospital which was cheaper and another step toward getting me out of the hospital and back home. My parents visited a few of the rehabilitation hospitals that were options for me and one of my physical therapists put in a call to the rehabilitation hospital that would be the best fit for me to try to help me get accepted. After a few days of having no idea when or where I was going, I was accepted into the rehabilitation hospital that my therapist recommended. The hospital had told my parents that I could stay there as long as I needed to as I couldn't go home until I could walk. The apartment I lived in was not wheelchair accessible; there were stairs to climb, no matter which floor I lived on.

CHAPTER 10

# Take a Seat

**John 8:25** *"'Who are you?' they asked. 'Just what I have been claiming all along,' Jesus replied."*

Just like every other hospital move, I was informed on the morning of the move. This was to be the fourth hospital I would be a patient in. I thanked all the people at the hospital and bid them farewell as I was wheeled out. As a parting gift, they put a pair of hospital scrub pants on me. It was a sign of normalcy as this was the first time I had worn pants since they had cut off the pants I had been wearing the day of the accident, ten weeks earlier. The ambulance arrived; I was loaded onto the gurney, put into the ambulance and driven about 30 minutes to the next hospital. I arrived at dinner time, and they transferred me into the bed from the gurney. Changing hospitals always caused anxiety. Who were my nurses, therapists and doctors going to be? I had just spent time building relationships with all the people at the previous hospital and now I had to start all over again. I had learned from the previous hospitals that it was important to build relationships with everyone that I interacted with regularly. All the people I encountered played a role in my care; they were the people who helped the insurance company to make decisions about how long I was going to stay in the hospital; they were the people who were going to help me recover. It was important that I advocated for myself and tell them my goals and what I was trying to accomplish. If they didn't know what my goals were then I might fall into the care plan that everyone else gets. The rehab hospital's goal was to get me out of the hospital, back home and able to function doing the basic tasks of life in whatever condition I was in; that was also my goal. But beyond that, I wanted to get my independence back; not just to get home, but also to rebuild my body back to what it once was, or as close as I could get, to how my body functioned before the crash.

I went to sleep not knowing what to expect. I was woken up by my new therapist the next morning at 7:00 AM. I opened my eyes to see a wheelchair next to my bed. I was told that it was time to wake up and get into my wheelchair. It was quite a shock; life had suddenly changed from being told not to move to being told that I would be taught how to transfer myself from my bed to my wheelchair. The reality of how difficult it was to move was apparent immediately. In order to get into the wheelchair, I had to first sit up. I hadn't been able to sit up on my own since the crash. It was probably the first time I had thought about what I needed to do to sit up since I was an infant trying to sit up for the first time. I had the same problem an infant has in their first efforts to sit up; a total lack of muscular strength. I was straining as hard as I could just to roll onto my side and sitting up with my current level of strength was not possible, no matter how hard I strained to sit up. After some help from the therapist getting onto my side, she showed me a short cut to sit up. If I moved my legs over the side of the bed, then gravity would help pull my legs to the ground and help to slowly pull my upper body into an upright position if I pulled hard enough on the handrails on the side of the bed. I couldn't count on my strength at that time, but I could still rely on gravity. My therapist then pulled out a two-foot-long shiny board that was about a foot wide. She put one end on the bed under my rear end and the other on the side of the wheelchair. She told me I had to slide myself on the board from the bed to the chair. I thought, *Does this seem safe?* I was scared of falling on the floor and rebreaking everything that was currently healing. I thought that this must be the way it was done;

I was sure I wasn't the first person who had to do this. After all, it is not like this was the most dangerous thing I had ever done. I tried to build up my belief that this was going to go well; I needed to commit to giving it all my energy to make it go well. I took a deep breath and committed to it. The therapist kept two hands on me while I tried to move. She had to pull me along most of the time as it was a real struggle. The short move was so difficult; not least of all because I wasn't allowed to put any weight on my legs because they were healing, and the doctors were afraid that any weight on my legs or pelvis could delay the healing process or cause additional damage. Without the strength from my legs, I had to rely completely on the strength of my upper body. My upper body had a total lack of strength as my arms had only been out of the casts for a few days. My greatest feat of strength, since the casts had been removed, had been opening the top of my yogurt container and that took two attempts. The therapist kept pulling me until I plopped into the chair. I was exhausted already. It took everything I had to move into the wheelchair and most of the work had been done by the therapist.

The therapist then asked me to wheel my chair to breakfast. I started to push the rails that moved the wheels. I had to get accustomed to coordinating all my muscles to push on those wheels since I hadn't used my muscles in ten weeks. The force I could generate to push the wheels was so low that the wheels didn't roll without me pushing them constantly; I was unable to build any momentum. Anytime I stopped pushing the wheels, the wheelchair stopped immediately. I also realized there was a big strength difference between my arms. My left arm was stuck in place at a 120-degree angle so that I could not straighten it or curl it up. I couldn't fully use all the muscles in that arm to propel myself forward so the wheelchair constantly veered to the left. I had to straighten the chair out by pushing only one wheel multiple times. I only made the chair move about ten feet before the therapist told me that she would take over and we would try this later. I read between the lines and what she was telling me was that if she let me push myself the whole way, breakfast time would be over as it only lasted an hour. As she wheeled me to the cafeteria, it hit me how difficult it was going to be to get my independence back again. It had taken every bit of energy, even with help, to get into the wheelchair and move the chair ten feet. I then reminded myself that this was just my starting point. Today was just what I was going to measure myself against tomorrow when I had to get out of bed and push my wheelchair again. I reminded myself that I just needed to get a little bit better each day and now I knew how to measure what a little bit better meant.

After getting back to my room that afternoon and going through the first day of rehabilitation, I thought I needed to do something to get a win for myself, to set the standard for what I was going to do every day going forward and set the tone for my rehabilitation. One of the things that concerned me about being sent to the rehabilitation hospital was whether I was ready for it. Up until that day, the longest I had been seated in the heavily padded wheelchair at the last hospital was two hours, and those two hours had been really painful. I usually had to be put back into my bed in under two hours because of the pain. I had doubts. How was I going to recover and become independent if I couldn't sit in a wheelchair for more than two hours without a huge amount of pain? I decided I was going to sit in my wheelchair as long as I possibly could that day. I was going to prove to myself that I could sit there for more than two hours. If I was going to recover, the most important part of recovery was that I had to believe I was capable of recovering. So, I sat in that chair from when I woke up and the therapist put me in it at 7:00 AM, until 8:00 PM that night. For most of the day, it was incredibly uncomfortable. All those muscles that hadn't been used were, all of a sudden, being asked to work more than they had since the crash. The muscles were weak and asking for relief, but I knew the only way they would stop asking for relief was to use them every day and build the strength back. My pelvis felt tender and uncomfortable all day, but sitting there was what it needed. Every few hours, the hospital staff would come in and ask me if I wanted to be put back into bed. I would thank them and tell them that I wanted to continue to sit in my chair. They had no idea why I insisted that I wanted to continue to sit in the chair when the bed seemed so much more comfortable. I wasn't looking for comfort; I know comfort was the enemy of rehabilitation. I was looking to recover, and I knew lying in the bed was the easy thing to do. I could take a nap if I wanted. I was even encouraged to take one. I was tired of taking naps. I was sick of lying in a bed. I was going to take advantage of everyday I was here. I was here to regain my independence.

The following morning, I was brought into my bathroom for a shower. I learned that day that I was unable to put on, or take off, my shirt on my own as I had lost a lot of flexibility in my arms and shoulders. I was able to sit up in the shower in my wheelchair however, which felt a little closer to normal than before when I had to lie down for a shower. I finished the shower with the assistance of my therapist. She placed me in front of the mirror that was in my bathroom. It was the first time I had looked in a mirror since the crash. I immediately saw my upper body. It was the first time I could see the scar that went from my clavicle down to my belt line. It was hard to look at. It felt like I was looking at someone else. I saw how all the muscle I had before the accident had withered away in the last two and a half months of lying in bed. I was just skin hanging on top of bone. It was shocking.

After looking at my arms and chest, I looked myself directly in the eyes; beyond the physical me into a much deeper level, and I asked myself, *Are you who you proclaim you are?* I always believed that I never knew how good I could be at anything I pursued until I pushed myself to an all-consuming, obsessive level; that unless I pushed myself to the breaking point, I would never really know how good I could be. I believed that anything I accomplished would be achieved by working harder than anyone else was willing to work. I believed that I performed my best when climbing mountains when my life was on the line and survival was not assured. Personal philosophies are typically developed when you are at your best, that high standard and lofty self-image of yourself is easier to live by when you are at your best. Was I willing to judge myself by my own lofty high standards while I was at my lowest? Could I live up to it? Was I who I proclaimed that I was or was the image I had of myself just that; an image made up in my own head? It wasn't something I could answer at that moment. It could only be answered through my actions going forward.

That afternoon, I continued my rehabilitation sessions, which amounted to about three and a half hours per day. Besides those three and half hours for rehab and three meals a day, I had a lot of free time. Those were hours I had to use to get better so I asked, on that second day, what exercises I could do on my own in my room. They handed me a list of exercises. I got back to my room that day and started doing those exercises. I wasn't sure how many to do; I determined that the more I did the better so I would finish the exercises, take a little break and do the exercises again. I would take another break and do them again. I started building a routine that I thought would bring me more independence, faster recovery and get me out of the hospital more quickly.

*My Mom took this picture of me the first time she entered my room in the ICU. I was in a coma. She took the picture just in case I didn't live she had one last picture of me.*

*This is the dent my body made when I crashed into the airplane hangar.*
*I took this picture the first time I revisited the crash site.*

*About a year before the crash after I landed my parachute*

*About a year before the crash. This was the first time I had a malfunction of my main parachute that could not be fixed. I cut the main parachute away and had to deploy the reserve parachute. The yellow parachute is the reserve parachute that I deployed and landed.*

*A quick photo before I spoke at Elizabeth United Methodist Church in Colorado*

*Sunrise on the Flatirons. Boulder, Colorado*

# CHAPTER 11

# The Goal

**James 2:26** *"As the body without the spirit is dead,*
*so faith without deeds is dead."*

The next day, I realized that the therapists had never asked me what my goals were. I had to advocate for myself and let them know what I expected out of rehabilitation and what I needed to get out of therapy so I could reach my goals. I told my therapists that I was going to walk out of the hospital when I was discharged. The therapists stared back at me like I was out of my mind. They didn't want to say that it wasn't possible and discourage me, but their faces told me they didn't believe in my goal. In retrospect, I can understand their skepticism. A few days earlier they had just watched how much effort it took for me to move from my bed to the wheelchair, and that was with a lot of assistance. They had witnessed me only being able to push the wheelchair about ten feet on my first attempt. They knew that typically, patients only get to stay in the rehab hospital for 3 weeks before they are sent home by the insurance company. They also knew that my last set of x-rays were taken just a few days before I had arrived, and the doctor would not allow me to put weight on my legs yet. I couldn't go back for additional x-rays for another month, so the insurance company would probably force me to leave the hospital before I could get cleared to put weight on my legs by the doctor. They see a lot of patients each year and based on their experience, they can usually predict what is possible and what isn't during the time the patient spends in rehab. I wasn't discouraged by the looks they gave me. I believed in what I said and had faith that I was going to walk out of the hospital. I was going to do the work and my body had to do the healing. The therapists would just guide me through it. It was my job to convince them that walking out was possible. It was my job to change the way they look at patients and what was possible.

A few days later, a hospital administrator came into my room and started to speak to me about being released from the hospital. I replied that I had just gotten there and asked why we were talking about being released. I told her that when we chose the hospital, my parents were told I could stay as long as I needed to and I wasn't going to be forced to leave in three weeks. I explained that I needed to walk out of the hospital as a wheelchair would not work where I lived because of the stairs. She explained that the release date was up to the insurance company and the hospital couldn't control what the insurance company decided.

I was concerned that I would be forced to leave the rehab hospital by the insurance company before I was able to go for my next set of leg and pelvis x-rays. I was concerned with what other options may be available. I had learned, from staying at various hospitals, that everything seemed to be a last minute decision. Each time I left the hospital I only received one day's notice and my family had to scramble to visit each potential hospital to figure which would be the best option. It felt like I was always on the verge of being pushed out of each hospital for a cheaper option. The constant short notice caused so much unnecessary stress. The insurance company had all the power; all the control of my care. Whatever decision they made was in their best interest and, as far as I could tell, was all in the name of saving money and preserving as much profit as possible. I may have been a paying customer, but the insurance company was a corporation; their priority was making a profit for their shareholders, not to make me better. I always kept that in mind. I tried to concentrate on controlling what I could control and trying not to worry about the insurance company and their decisions as I had no control over that. I was on some unknown timetable of getting out of the hospital, but no one would commit to what the timeframe was. What I did know was that a patient had to show progress each week as the hospital had to report to the insurance company. If I stopped improving, they would force the hospital to discharge me. I knew what I needed to do was to get better every week, as I had control of that, and hope that the insurance company would keep approving me to stay longer.

The following day, I sprang into action. My therapist woke me up for my therapy session at 7:00 AM. The times of the sessions were never consistent; sometimes you were woken up before breakfast for a therapy session and other times they might start at 10:00. You never knew ahead of time. I suppose I was a captive audience. I was going to be in my room no matter what time they showed up. When my therapist woke me up, I mentioned the conversation I had with the hospital administrator the day before and my concern that I would be released before I could go back to the orthopedic doctors for my next set of x-rays on my legs. I reminded her I needed to be cleared by the doctors before I could walk and I needed to walk before I left the hospital. As soon as I got that out, I could tell she wasn't in the mood to have this unloaded on her at 7:00 AM. She raised her voice and snapped back at me saying she didn't have control over when I would be released. As soon as she snapped at me, I backed off. I needed her on my side, not mad at me. She wheeled me down to the room where the rehab sessions took place, and I stayed quiet the entire time to give her a breather. We started going through the first exercises for the day. In a break between exercises, I apologized for upsetting her. I explained how much I needed her help if I was ever going to get better and I needed her help with whatever she could do to convince the insurance company to keep me there as long as possible so I could walk out of the hospital. I told her I would do my part to get a little better each week. Suddenly her body language and her whole demeanor changed. Maybe she hadn't been told by her patients how important she was often enough. Maybe she finally heard what she needed to hear; that she was important and that she was helping to change people's lives for the better and the patients really needed her help to achieve their goals. From then on, she was on my side. I did my part by getting a little better each week, she helped me get better and did what she could with her reports to the insurance company to convince them to keep me in the hospital.

CHAPTER 12

# The Long Walk Home

**Isaiah 41:10** *"So do not fear, for I am with you; do not be dismayed, for I am your God. I will strengthen and help you; I will uphold you with my righteous right hand."*

Each day, I was progressing a little bit more. I judged that by how far I could push my wheelchair. I finally was able to go outside for the first time. Other than the short time I spent outside during my transfers to and from the ambulance for visits to the orthopedic doctors, which happened once a month, I hadn't spent any time outdoors. I could now push my wheelchair outside around the building. It was nice to have the sun shining on my face for the first time since the crash. It always improved my mood as I loved the outdoors. I continued to work out in my room each day, on my own. The physical therapists started noticing that I was working out in my room every time they walked in. They started giving me new exercises to do and would bring in equipment from the gym to help me do additional exercises on my own. Maybe some of those therapists started to believe I could possibly walk out of there on my last day. Even if they didn't believe, they appeared willing to feed into my own delusion that I was going to walk out. Either way, I really didn't care because they were providing me with the help I needed to reach my goal.

By this point, I had done about as much therapy as I could do on my upper body and as much work in the wheelchair as I could. I was showing improvement each week, so I was able to stay. I just needed to stay until I could get my next set of x-rays; if I could put weight on my legs then I could potentially stay longer to learn how to walk again. The big day was finally approaching to get my next set of x-rays. Would I be going home in a wheelchair or to some nursing home until I could use my legs or was I finally going to be able to stand and put weight on my legs?

The ambulance came to pick me up and it was the first time I was able to ride in an ambulance sitting up in my wheelchair. It was my first view of the outside world other than the outside of the rehab building when I was pushing my wheelchair. The day was bright and sunny, without a cloud in the sky. As we drove west, I finally saw a view of the mountains, for the first time in over 3 months. The view of the mountains and the sunshine gave me hope for the upcoming appointment. I finally got my x-rays done and I was sitting in the doctor's office waiting for the results. The next few minutes would determine the direction I was going to go in for the next few months. The doctor reviewed the x-rays in front of me and turned to me and said, "Your pelvis and leg are not fully healed, but they are healed enough that you can put weight on them and start trying to walk." He explained that putting some weight on them would help with the healing process. I finally got the good news I had been waiting for. I felt a huge weight lift off my shoulders. I felt like I was going to have more control in my rehabilitation because I got the green light to try to walk. Getting the green light was not something I could control, but being able to walk was in my control. I then asked the doctor when he thought I would be able to run again. He paused for a minute and was lost for words. He looked back at me like he couldn't believe I asked him that question. I suppose he wasn't expecting that to be the next logical question I would ask after he just cleared me to put weight on my legs. He took a minute to think about how he wanted to respond and said, "You may never be able to run again, the pain may be too much." I took his statement as a challenge. I never believed that what he said was correct. I was going to run again. I stored his statement about not being able to run again in the back of my mind for later use. For now, I needed to focus on learning to walk again.

The ambulance headed back to the rehab hospital and the mountains were glowing from the sunlight. I couldn't wait to get back. I returned just in time for lunch and started to eat. About halfway through lunch, the news reached my therapist that I had returned, and that I was going to be able to try to walk. She came into the cafeteria and asked me if I wanted to try to walk. I dropped my fork and turned to her and said, "Let's go!" She wheeled me to the rehab room. The anticipation of walking for the first time in over three months gave me the same feeling I would normally get when I was skydiving; the feeling I got when the plane had reached the altitude that we were going to jump from and the door was opened.

My therapist put my wheelchair between two parallel bars that were there to support my arms in case I needed them to stabilize myself. She asked me to stand up. I scooted my butt to the edge of the seat, planted my feet and pushed up. I slowly started to rise out of the seat. My legs were shaking uncontrollably just from the effort to stand up. I finally managed to stand all the way up. It was the first time I had been completely upright since jumping out of the plane. It felt so good to stand up for the first time. I had been visualizing what it would be like every day since I started training my mind. The therapist then told me to try to walk. I took one small step and then another. My legs were shaking from the effort, but I was walking. After a few steps, the therapist put the wheelchair under me again and let me sit down and rest while she moved the chair back to the start of the parallel bars again. I repeated the six foot walk two more times. The therapist told me that I had done enough for the first day as she didn't want to overwork me the first day I could walk.

My therapist wheeled me back to my room in my wheelchair. She remarked that I didn't look that happy after walking. I suppose she assumed I would be celebrating. She said, "I have been doing this for 15 years and I have never seen someone with all of your injuries and not being able to walk for three months get up and walk like you just walked." I turned toward her and reminded her that my goal wasn't to walk a few steps but to walk out of the hospital when I was released; this was just the first step.

Just as my goal in the beginning of rehab was to push my wheelchair a little bit further each day, my new goal was to walk a little bit further each day. They presented me with a walker the next day. Just like my first day trying to push the wheelchair to the cafeteria, my therapist tried to have me walk to the cafeteria for breakfast. I got about 100 feet before they put me back in the wheelchair and pushed me the rest of the way there. I wished I could have walked further, but this was just the first day and this first day was what I would measure myself against tomorrow when I was going to walk a little further.

Each day I walked a little bit further than the day before. My therapist said they were thinking about releasing me in the next three days. After only walking for two days, I asked if they could keep me for another week. I think they were surprised that I asked to stay longer. On the one hand, I wanted to go home and sleep in my own bed and couldn't wait to get out of the hospital; but on the other hand, I knew if they sent me home and I wasn't able to walk more than a few steps, it would be difficult to get around and a therapist would only come to my home two days a week for one hour. I would only get two sessions a week which would slow down my progress. I convinced them that if they kept me another week, I would get at least three hours of therapy a day for that week; the equivalent of ten weeks worth of at home therapy in one week, just by staying in the hospital. In addition, I had had a few missteps in my walking thus far and I would have fallen without the therapist being next to me and holding onto to me to keep me from falling. The last thing I wanted to do was fall and break my pelvis and leg again. Luckily, they were able to convince the insurance company to keep me one more week.

I continued to walk longer distances each day and I learned how to climb stairs again. I traded my walker in for a set of crutches. The crutches seemed like a much more natural way to walk. I learned how to get up from the floor. I had never thought of that until now. I was so inflexible and weak that I wasn't sure if I got on the floor at home to do exercises if I would be able to get back up. I gained confidence when they showed me a new technique to get up that took less flexibility and strength than the normal way I would get up prior to the injuries.

I started to plan what I would do once I got home from the hospital. No one sits you down and plans your next steps of recovery. I found out during this recovery process there were a lot of things that I needed to figure out myself. No matter how great my therapists and the hospital staff were while I was there, they didn't have enough time or resources to really guide me down a path of recovery. I could always ask questions while I was in a therapy session or when a nurse or doctor was in my room, but sometimes I didn't even know what question to ask. I had never been through any process like this before and I only knew what I knew. The instructions for when I got home were to find a therapist that my insurance company covered and start scheduling sessions. I asked for recommendations and didn't get any. I looked up therapists on my insurance company's website and started to research them but the information available was woefully inadequate. I knew picking the right therapist once I got out of the hospital was of the utmost importance; they would guide my recovery from then on. It was time for me to take control of planning my recovery and steer the ship. It was up to me, once I stepped out of this hospital, to plan and direct everything that needed to be done. Taking control back, after feeling at the mercy of someone else planning all my care, felt empowering.

In my search for a therapist, I found what seemed to be a highly rated therapy center that was located at a university 3 miles from where I lived. After speaking to them and trying to schedule an appointment, they told me that they didn't take people as broken as I was. I was taken back by that comment. *Too broken*, I thought. Well, it was their loss. I was determined to find someone else who would help. I looked up the orthopedic group that performed all the surgeries on my broken bones.

I figured if they were willing to be there in my darkest hours to fix my body, those are the kind of people that I needed to see for my therapy. I called and they scheduled my first appointment for two days after I left the hospital.

I began to plan my workout routine for when I got home. I thought four hours a week of therapy with a physical therapist was not nearly enough if I was going to recover at the speed I wanted to recover. I started writing down all the exercises that I had been doing in my daily session with the therapists and then included all the exercises that I had been doing on my own. I started thinking of all the time I spent in the gym over the years and the exercises I did. I identified the exercises that I had the ability to do now, in my current state, to build my strength. I didn't dwell on exercises I couldn't do. I knew I had to start somewhere. If I ever wanted to get back to being independent, I had to start with what I could do now; that would eventually allow me to build up to the exercises I needed to get me back to where I wanted to be. I organized all the training into multiple sessions that would be completed each day, along with the physical therapy appointments I would go to four times a week. I built in time to walk outside each day, which would allow me to work on my endurance and to spend time outside, which I missed so much while I was in the hospital.

During that last week in the hospital, a new nurse was assigned to me. He came in, introduced himself and asked how I was feeling. I replied that I was okay, then I asked how he was doing. He looked at me with a surprised look and said, "No one ever asks me that. Thank you for asking." I could tell he was having a hard day. We started talking and he started opening up to me. He told me that one of the most difficult things about his job is that he spends so much time taking care of patients and he never knows how their lives turn out once they leave the hospital. He never knows if his contribution to their recovery made a difference or not. After he left my room, I reflected on all the people that had helped me. If he was questioning how much of a difference he makes in the lives of his patients, there must be others struggling with this as well. I promised myself that after I made enough progress in my rehabilitation at home, I would return to the hospitals where I had stayed to show the people who helped me what a difference they made in my life and to thank them for everything they did for me so they knew everything they do, every day, can restore people and allow them to return to their normal, everyday lives.

A day before I was scheduled to leave the hospital, that same nurse came in before he finished his shift; he had stopped by to check on me. He wished me good luck with my ongoing recovery once I left; he shared with me that he had been in a snowboarding accident a few years earlier and had broken his back. He said he had had to wear a brace and had been unable to leave his couch for four months. He said one thing he learned from that experience, that he wanted to pass on to me, was to not let this accident stop me from doing things I want to do in life. He knew I was active and did all kinds of outdoor sports. He told me to still take chances and not to let what happened in this accident hold me back.

The following day, I woke up and prepared to leave the hospital. I ate breakfast and thanked all the people who worked in the cafeteria. The quality of food that they provided in the hospital allowed me to finally start eating normally again and helped my body recover. It was amazing how much eating great tasting food put me in a good mood and gave me the energy to repair my body and the energy to go through physical therapy.

Check out time was quickly approaching. My Dad came to the hospital to pick me up. It had been ten days since I had been allowed to take those first few steps, but the hospital had never cleared me to walk on my own. They would only allow me to walk while a therapist was standing next to me. I suppose there was going to be a first time for everything, because I was about to walk on my own without anyone there to catch me if I fell. I received my final discharge instructions, and then it was time to leave. The hospital was always quiet on the weekends as none of the therapists work on the weekends and only the essential staff are there. It was time to go. I stood up, put the crutches under my arms and walked out of the hospital and all the way to the car, just like I had told my therapists I would 40 days earlier.

CHAPTER 13

# Driven

**James 1:12 CSB** *"Blessed is a man who endures trials, because when he passes the test he will receive the crown of life that He has promised to those who love Him."*

My Dad drove the 50 miles back home. As we crested the last hill and descended into town, the Flatirons were illuminated by the sun the same way they had been on the morning of the crash. It had been three and a half months since I had laid my eyes on the Flatirons and their amazing beauty. It felt like that glow of the sun hitting the Flatirons was welcoming me home.

Coming home was going to be another challenge. The safety net was gone. If I fell while I was walking, there wasn't going to be anyone to catch me. If something didn't feel right with my body, there wasn't anyone down the hall who could come in and check on me. It didn't matter whether I felt ready or not; this was the situation going forward.

Over the first few days at home, I adjusted to having to shower with no one helping me, cooking my own food and doing the everyday normal tasks that someone does when they are not in the hospital. I went to the supermarket for the first time to buy food and tried to resume what I remembered as a normal life. Everything took much more effort than it had before the crash. Each time I got off the couch, I would strategically plan everything I needed to do while I was walking around beforehand as just standing up was an arduous task that required a lot of energy.

My parents had been at my side for the last three and a half months and had handled so many things while I was in the hospital. They tried to take as much off my plate as possible so all I had to worry about was healing and rehabilitating my body. They had to be exhausted from all they had to deal with each day and they had been away from their own home for three and half months. They had done so much; I wanted them to be able to return to their normal life. I told them that I thought it was time that they went back to their normal life. It was time for me to fend for myself. If I was ever going to get better, I needed to make my life uncomfortable. I needed to do everything myself. They volunteered to help me each time they saw me struggle to stand up to get a drink, cook or wash dishes, but I needed to do those things for myself. I needed to isolate myself and get to work. The best way to gauge how determined I was to get better was to isolate myself and see how much work I was willing to put into recovery. It was going to be a long process of repeating the same exercises every day for months on end with the goal of just getting a fraction of a percentage better each day.

I didn't want to hear the compliments that I was doing so well or reassurances about how much progress I had made. I needed to tap into the negative comments that people had made like: "You may never run again" or the psychiatrist trying to tempt me to take the easy road by taking the antidepressants or the look on the face of my therapists when I told them I was going to walk out of the rehab hospital. I knew being alone would test my determination to recover from my injuries. Being alone can bring your weaknesses to the forefront but being alone can also allow you to show your true strength. Being alone provides no counterbalance when you are doubting yourself but also provides no limit on my expectations regarding what is possible for me to achieve, regardless of whether my expectations were realistic or not.

Just as the coma tested me when I was isolated in darkness and seclusion; when the temptation came, I had to decide whether it was worth fighting to stay alive or not. Being on my own at home would make me confront temptation. Was the recovery that I made so far good enough? Was I capable of more? How badly did I want to run again? How much improvement did I want to show my family, friends and the people who had helped me in the hospital when I returned to visit?

My parents were reluctant to leave; they were concerned that I could not get around enough on my own to take care of myself. They were also concerned about my mental well-being after this life changing experience I had been through. I proved to them that I could take care of myself over the first few days of being home and they reluctantly returned to their own lives.

After they left, I started to get to work on rehabbing my body. I would get up, eat breakfast and then start. I would work out eight to ten hours a day, seven days a week, doing various exercises to loosen up my body which had become so tight during my recovery. I would go walk outside and I started lifting light weights at home. Then, I would go to my therapy session with my new therapists. Doing rehab was like having a full-time job. I needed to get better, and I was going to take advantage of every day.

# CHAPTER 14

# Survivor's Guilt

**Psalm 91:4-6** *"He will cover you with his feathers, and under his wings you will find refuge; his faithfulness will be your shield and rampart. You will not fear the terror of night, nor the arrow that flies by day, nor the pestilence that stalks in darkness, nor the plague that destroys at midday."*

Throughout my entire stay in the hospital, I had looked forward to getting out and visiting the people at the drop zone, the place where people skydive, who had helped me on the day of the crash. I especially wanted to thank the person whose voice I had heard while I was lying on the ground after the crash. I knew exactly whose voice it was. It was one of my instructors who had helped teach me to skydive a few years earlier. I was planning to visit once my walking endurance improved. I had been on social media a few days after getting home and saw a go fund me page for that instructor. Just a week earlier, he had been in a terrible skydiving accident, which left him with a traumatic brain injury. The prognosis was that he would never fully recover. I couldn't believe what I was reading. I felt like the wind had been knocked out of me. Two weeks later, another skydiver that I had jumped with on a few occasions died in an accident. I questioned why I was so lucky. Why was I spared from death, a traumatic brain injury or any spinal damage? I had survivor's guilt. Why did I get a second chance and they didn't?

A few weeks later, I returned to the drop zone. I felt like my recovery process should include confronting what had happened. I needed to revisit where I had almost met my end. I showed up on a day in early November, a Friday, which was one of the quieter days of the week for jumping. I wasn't sure how I was going to react to being there and I didn't want to be overwhelmed by seeing too many people at once. I thanked the safety manager, and everyone else who had helped me that day. From the person who called 911 and kept watch over me until the ambulance carted me away, to the people who had to call my emergency contact to give them the terrible news, to the person who was willing to bring my car to my family after the crash so they had use of my car while I was in a coma. I also apologized if I had given any of them PTSD as I can't imagine seeing what they saw that day or what it must have been like to call my friend to inform her of the crash. I felt overwhelmed and so happy to see those smiling faces and appreciated all the hugs they gave me. I couldn't say thank you enough. Saying thank you felt so inadequate as a payment for how much they had helped me.

After saying thank you to everyone I knew, I had to go to the site of the accident. I headed for the landing area and the building that I had crashed into. I first looked at the fence that I had ripped through. The metal wires were still lying on the ground. The two poles that formerly held the wired fence were still in the ground; the posts were marked with old sneakers upside down on top of the stakes. I then looked at the building, which was about ten feet behind the fence. The side of the building had a huge dent in it where my body had made impact. I took a picture of the dent. I stared at the landing area, looked up at the sky and stood there for about five minutes. I thought I might breakdown or get upset but my mood didn't really change. I was quiet and thought, *This is the place where I almost died.* I looked around for a few minutes. I thought of the two people who had recently been in those horrible accidents on this same field who didn't have the chance to walk away. I got back into my car and headed home. Part of my recovery was to revisit what happened; not to avoid anything that might be uncomfortable. As I quietly headed home, I thought about how very lucky I was to have a second chance and I needed to get back to work on my recovery.

That night, after finishing my rehab, I went to take a shower. Each time I took a shower I would get undressed and look at myself in the bathroom mirror. I would see all the scars and it felt like I was looking at someone else. It took time to fully accept that this was my body now. That day, for the first time, I accepted that this was the new me. For good or bad, this was me. I needed to start being proud of what I looked like. I had to start loving those scars as they were part of me, and they weren't going away. If nothing else, they helped tell my story.

A few weeks later, I had finally built up the confidence to join a gym. For the first time since the accident, I was going to be on display to the general public. This was no longer the gym at the rehabilitation center. I was going to mix with normal people. One of the reasons I wanted to go to the gym was because there was a pool there. When I was in the water, I moved around freely, without a care in the world. I could use my body the way I had before the accident. Swimming made me feel like I had no injuries. When I was in the water, it gave me a preview of how I hoped my body would function again after I recovered.

I was reminded that this wasn't a rehab gym when I walked to the pool the first day without a towel draped over my upper body. It was just my crutches and my giant zipper scar that went from my clavicle to my belt line, and it was red and fresh looking. No one said anything or asked any questions, but I could feel the eyes staring at me and gawking. You could tell they wanted to know what had happened as someone in their early 40s typically doesn't have a scar like that. I could care less if they stared; I was comfortable with my body now. I wore my scars with pride. I would just smile, walk and think to myself, *Stare all you want, this is what a genetic freak of nature looks like.*

On one of my first days in the gym, I decided to work on my leg strength. I crawled under a bar to do squats. I chose a bar that had a fixed range of motion so I could hold it on my shoulders without the risk of dropping it as my left arm was still fixed in place and could not hold the bar. I decided to start with no weight on the bar to warm up. I wanted to stay conservative. After doing ten repetitions I realized I wasn't going to be adding any weight as just the bar with no weight was extremely difficult. For a few seconds I was deflated. I couldn't believe this was all I could lift. *Just the bar?* Then I decided this wasn't a day I wanted to forget, this was a day to remember because this was a day that I was going to look back on months from now when I could lift a lot more weight. I would look back at this same bar and remember the day I could only lift the bar with no weight on it.

CHAPTER 15

# Crutches

**Isaiah 40:29** *"He gives strength to the weary and increases the power of the weak."*

Weeks passed and I was making gains in strength and endurance. One of my mottos was, *Remove all crutches.* Whether it was a mental crutch, a medication I still had to take, a self-imposed limitation or a literal crutch, I wanted to walk without having any devices aiding me. Little by little, I went from having two crutches, to one crutch, to a cane and then, eventually, walking short distances without any support. I would walk every day. I was so grateful to be moving in the upright position that I didn't want to go a day without using my legs. The more I walked, the stronger my legs got. I never let anything get in the way of walking every day. There were days when I encountered freezing rain which soaked me to the bone. There was a day when it was snowing, with temperatures below zero degrees, and no one else was on a popular trail where I often saw dozens of people. I was shivering, cold and uncomfortable. The desolation of the trail and the fact that I didn't see anyone else on the trail that day was confirmation enough for me that I was heading in the right direction; I was supposed to be out walking that day.

I was doing the same exercises over and over, day after day, week after week, and the improvements I was making each day were so small it was difficult to track my progress. Was all this hard work helping? I decided I needed something to measure my progress. A clock doesn't lie. Whether the time was faster or slower than the last time I tested myself would let me know where I stood. I found a trail that went in a loop. It was a loop that I would have never run on before the accident because it was too short but at the speed that I was currently moving, it took a long time and a big effort to get around that loop. Each time I would walk around the loop I would time myself to gauge my progress. Week after week, the time it took me to complete the loop went down. Rehab was working. The more the time went down, the more I looked forward to getting back to work and training for that next time I tested myself.

Early December approached and I had to go in for another surgery. My left arm had been stuck at a 120-degree angle since the crash. My elbow had been dislocated and fractured in the crash and that, combined with the concussion I had, resulted in heterotopic ossification in my elbow. When I hit my head, my brain was confused into creating additional bone in my elbow that it didn't need. The result was that I could not bend my elbow at all in either direction; it was stuck in a fixed position. To repair this, my surgeon opened my elbow back up and, with a hammer and chisel, broke off pieces of bone until my elbow joint regained some mobility. While breaking bone, my elbow tendon had been cut 90 percent of the way through, so the doctor decided to help strengthen the damaged tendon by weaving in a cadaver tendon with my tendon.

I was back to walking by the second day after surgery and back to the gym three days after surgery. I decided to start lifting weights with the surgically repaired arm three days after surgery. My physical therapist casually asked me what I had been doing since the surgery and I told her I had been lifting light weights with it at the gym; at which point she started yelling at me. She said that she had not given me permission to lift weights. She yelled, "You just had surgery on Monday!" I remembered her instruction before the surgery was to move my arm after the surgery. I may have stretched her definition of "move" a bit and she may have been right as I had heard cracking noises in my elbow when I picked up the weight; but being able to move my heavily bandaged elbow, even just an inch, was too much for me to resist. My response to her was that if I asked permission every time I did something new during my rehab, I wouldn't be as far along. I was a little shocked that she had yelled at me, but I know it was out of concern; she was an amazing therapist and always looked out for me.

A week after the surgery, I visited my other orthopedic surgeon to x-ray my leg again. He looked at my leg and pelvis and told me they were completely healed. I asked him if I could try running. He looked at me with that same crazy look that my other orthopedic doctor had given me when he had x-rayed me three months earlier, before he cleared me to walk for the first time. He was quiet for about 30 seconds and then he said "If you want to try, that is okay. Your leg won't feel like it is your leg at first." I took that as a ringing endorsement that I should try to run right away. My walking wasn't very stable at this point, but if he said I could run, then I should try. Sometimes you hear what you want to hear. He did say I could run although he said it cautiously, without much conviction.

I headed home from the doctor's office and on the way home I remembered three months earlier, when I first got cleared to try to walk for the first time. I remembered the gift the doctor gave me when he said I might never run again. I knew as soon as I got home what I needed to do. I started running. It was more like a hobble than a run as my legs and pelvis were still so tight and bound up from the crash but for where I was at this point, I will call it a run. I'm glad I was not in front of a mirror to see what I looked like. I went 50 feet and stopped. This was my starting point. I vowed to add another 50 feet to the run each day.

CHAPTER 16

# Jell-O

**1 Thessalonians 5:18** *"Give thanks in all circumstances, for this is God's will for you in Christ Jesus."*

After running a few times, I finally felt like I had made enough progress to return to the hospitals where I had spent so much time to show all the people who had helped me how much further along I was in my recovery, thanks to their help. I had promised myself that I would show everyone the progress I had made after my nurse in the rehab hospital told me the hardest part of his job was not knowing what happened to the patients after they left the hospital. The first place I chose to visit was the hospital where I had had all my surgeries; the one I was flown to by the Flight for Life helicopter. It was the hospital where I had been the least coherent and most medicated, so I had the fewest clear memories once I woke up from the coma. My clearest memories were of all the nightmares I had during the coma, the nightmares I had after waking up from the coma and the panic attacks that woke me up every night.

I drove to the hospital and parked outside. I had to take a few minutes to sit in the car to compose myself. I was headed up to the ICU to visit those amazing people who had taken care of me when I was barely surviving. I got off the elevator, which left me in a quiet waiting room that was completely empty. My legs started to feel weak, like Jell-O. My weakness

87

had nothing to do with my injuries; they were a reaction to my current emotional state. I had to sit down and compose myself. I felt extremely nervous. What was I going to say? Would they remember me? I was so nervous I had to go to the bathroom twice within five minutes. It was the same nervous feeling as when I completed my first 15 or 20 skydives. I got out of the bathroom for the second time and sat down again. I finally gathered the nerve to get up and open the door to the ICU. I went to the nurse's station and handed the nurse a box of chocolates and tried to introduce myself but I stumbled over my words. I took a deep breath and explained why I was there and who I was. Telling people that I was the skydiver who crashed into a building always jogged people's memories; they must not know a ton of skydivers who had crashed into buildings. The nurse said she was surprised that I came back to visit because no one ever comes back to the ICU to visit. Once she said that, I knew I had made the right decision to visit, no matter how hard it was to get off the couch in the waiting room and open that door. These people needed to know how important they are. I thanked the nurse and asked if any of the nurses that watched over me were working that day. She called down to the other nurse's station and the nurse she called told her to send me down to her. I felt a sense of familiarity as soon as I walked down to the nurse's station. I could not recognize the nurse's face, but I remembered her long, blonde hair. I had been heavily medicated and spaced out when I was in the ICU but I remembered her leaning over me, taking care of my bandages and removing some of the tubes that drained blood from my body; I remembered her hair. When I got to her station, she came around the desk and gave me a hug. She remembered me and confirmed it by recounting conversations that we had while I was in the ICU. I didn't remember the conversations but, based on the detail she remembered from our conversations, it was obvious that she remembered me. The details she recounted about the crash were details that only I could have known. I got choked up when she was talking to me; saying thank you wasn't enough. I asked her which room I had stayed in. She pointed it out and there was no one currently using the room, so I walked in and stood there for a minute or two. So much had happened in that room. The nightmares, the fighting for my life, the doctor staring at me because he couldn't understand how I was alive, squeezing my Mom's hand while I was in the coma, taking my first drink of water when I woke up; seeing the sun for the first time after eight days of darkness. I walked out of the room, thanked the nurse again and walked out of the ICU. I went out to my car and sat in it for a while, just staring at the hospital. I finally started my car and drove around the outside of the hospital and saw where the Flight for Life helicopter was perched on its landing pad. I had unknowingly started a tradition that any time I am in the area of the hospital I drive around the perimeter of the hospital and think about how much all of those people did for me while I was there and I say thank you.

I returned home from the hospital and started writing thank you notes to doctors, therapists and nurses who had helped me. I wrote thank you letters to the ambulance companies, the paramedics and the fire company that brought me to the hospital, my friends who had come to visit me and my skydiving friends who had raised money for me. I wrote notes to my siblings who helped me so much and to my parents who had been there the entire time. I continued to visit the other hospitals over the next few weeks to thank them and show them I could, in fact, walk and that I did look a little bit better after a shower and in normal clothes, rather than a hospital gown.

# CHAPTER 17

# Destroy All Timeframes

**2 Timothy 1:7** *"For God did not give us a spirit of timidity, but a spirit of power, of love and of self-discipline."*

My next step was to return to work. My disability payments were not going to last forever. I felt a need to return to normal life. I couldn't just use every day for rehabilitation for the remainder of my life. Part of the draw may have been to see if I could perform at a high level at work again. I hadn't worked in 7 months. I definitely had my doubts. Could I remember everything I knew how to do? Would the stress be too much for me to handle? Did I actually want to go back to the place that I blamed for setting me on a path that I felt so much regret for after the crash? I had the best of intentions of going back and putting what I learned into action to make sure I didn't make the same mistakes again but having the best of intentions and actually executing on not getting sucked up in working too many hours are two different things. I needed to make sure I could keep some sort of balance in life because I hadn't fought so hard to live just to perform my job again. My job was there to sustain me and pay for my needs, but I couldn't allow myself to get sucked back into that solitary life of work, work, work. I had a purpose in life again and I needed to make sure I was going to fulfill my reason for getting a second chance. God had a plan for me, and it wasn't to go back to the same habits and lifestyle that I had before the crash. I needed to keep my eye on the reason why I lived.

I sat in my office chair for the first time since the crash, and it took weeks to just get accustomed to sitting there all day. My body would ache; I would get tired just from being there all day. Each time I got out of my chair, it took a few minutes of walking to loosen up my body enough to stand up straight again. Many days, I had to go home and go right to sleep as it really would wear me out physically to get through the day. I continued to go to physical therapy in the morning, before work, to help my recovery.

The sun started setting later and for the first time, I decided to go outside to run/hobble. I was moving away from the safe hallway I had been running/hobbling in. I decided I would alternate between running for 30 seconds and walking for two minutes for the first workout. It took about 20 minutes before I stopped limping; it took a long time to loosen the muscles around my legs and pelvis. I would go out and complete my running workout every other day. With each passing week, I would run a little longer and walk a little less. After three weeks, I tried to figure out what I thought I would be capable of doing by the summer. I wondered if I would be able to enter a stroke and stride race in June. A stroke and stride race consists of a swim of 750 or 1500 meters and a five kilometer run. It was an event that I had participated in lots of times after work, in preparation for racing triathlons when I had been racing them often, six years previously. I calculated how much I needed to increase the distance I ran each week to build up to 5K by June. I then needed to start swimming again. Luckily, the week before, my physical therapist had given me her approval to go back into the pool and swim again. I then calculated how long I thought it would take me to build up to a 1500-meter swim. I convinced myself it was possible to do the stroke and stride in June and I signed up for the race right away. That set a deadline for me to accomplish what I needed to do to show up and be able to complete the distance within the time limit. Was it possible to finish in the time limit? There was only one way I would find out.

I had a conversation with my Mom and I let her know about the stroke and stride. She was a bit surprised that I had already signed up for a short race; she was always concerned that I would hurt myself if I started trying to progress too quickly. I always brushed off her concern as her just being my concerned mother. When I talked to her this time, she finally explained why she was concerned. She told me that early on, after I woke up from the coma and the doctors knew I would live, the doctors took my family aside and told my family that they thought I wouldn't walk for at least six months and I wouldn't go back to work for at least a year. My family never told me about any of those predictions as they may have made me incredibly depressed; I was very fragile in those early days after waking up. Because I didn't know about the predictions the doctors had made, I had expected to be fully healed every time I went for x-rays while I was in the hospital. I was always impatient to heal. I was always trying to think of something else I could do to hasten my recovery. It was a good thing that I hadn't known about the predictions; I set my own goals and had my own expectations for healing; whether they were realistic or not, I did not care.

After having that conversation with my Mom, I was out running/hobbling the following day and I was thinking about the doctor's prediction that I wouldn't walk for at least six months. The prediction was wrong because I walked in 3 months. The doctor said I wouldn't go back to work for more than a year and I went back in seven months. The doctor who fixed my pelvis said I may never be able to run again. What was I capable of doing if I didn't put limitations on myself?

I did another week of training and I convinced myself that the stroke and stride wasn't enough. I needed to up the stakes. I needed to prove to myself what I was capable of. I wanted to try to complete a triathlon. Months earlier, a few days after waking up from the coma on one of those quiet nights alone, I had set a goal for myself to do a triathlon again. It would signify to me that my arms, legs and heart worked again. I had initially set the goal for two years after the accident. I didn't tell anyone that this was a goal of mine as I didn't know quite what the reaction would be. I knew how my brain worked and I knew I needed a goal to shoot for. It would be a measurement of the progress that I made. The beautiful thing about a triathlon is either I complete it, or I don't. Either I finished within the time limits set by the race director, or I didn't. I would enter the race as a normal individual. I didn't want any exceptions or special treatment. I would race under the same standards everyone else raced under.

My rationale was that if I had recovered in half the time the doctors predicted, then why should I limit myself and settle for doing a triathlon in two years if I could potentially do one in 1 year? Was it possible? I couldn't be sure unless I committed to doing it. The doubt in my mind of whether it was possible was too much for me to resist. My brother Greg would tell me, "Destroy everyone's predicted timeframes for your recovery"; that meant even my own predictions. I remembered a race I had competed in 7 years earlier. It occurred in June and when I checked the date, it fell 1 day short of the one year anniversary of the crash. I signed up for the race. Now I had my goal and a new timeframe in which to accomplish it.

The following day, I got my bike out and went outside with it for the first time since the crash. I had three months to train for the race. It was going to be tough. I was starting from a fitness level of zero and I was still rehabilitating my injuries and going to outpatient rehab twice a week. I was far from fully functioning; but the challenge was set. I needed to get as fit as possible in three months so I could meet the time cutoffs of the race. I was under no illusion that I would be able to go fast or race like I did before the crash at this stage. Getting to the finish line in the time allotted would be my challenge.

CHAPTER 18

# Into the Storm

**Deuteronomy 10:21** *"He is your praise; he is your God, who performed for you those great and awesome wonders you saw with your own eyes."*

The day finally arrived in early June to do the stroke and stride as a tune up for my upcoming triathlon. This would be an important indicator of how my training had been going and could predict if I was close to being ready for the triathlon. This would be the first time I did an open water swim in a lake in six years. The starting gun sounded; I started swimming and got about 100 yards from shore before I started having a panic attack. My heart rate was over 200 beats per minute, I was hyperventilating and gasping for breath. The only time I had had panic attacks previously was when I had been in the hospital in those first few weeks after waking up from the coma. I was instantly transported back into that hospital room, gasping for breath and waking up from one of those terrible nightmares. I turned on my back and tried to gather myself and catch my breath. Had I made a mistake by rushing back into attempting a race? When I turned over on my back, I was looking directly at the beach. I knew I could just turn around and go back to shore and give up, but I had come too far to turn around, too far to take the easy way out, too far to choose comfort over being uncomfortable.

I took a few deep breaths and tried to calm down. I turned back over to my stomach and started to swim again. I could tell you that I turned over and started swimming the way I knew I could swim but the truth is that it was a struggle. It felt like I was going so slowly that the lifeguards were going to stop me and tell me I couldn't finish because I was taking too long. It turned out, when I got to shore, it wasn't as bad as I thought. It wasn't fast, but I managed to finish the 750 meter swim. I transitioned to the run/hobble. I saw someone 50 yards in front of me and I was trying to catch up to the person. I couldn't figure out how I wasn't catching up to a person who was alternating between walking and running while I was running the entire time. I finally figured out why after I finished the race. I looked at my watch and realized how slowly I had been running. After I finished, I realized this upcoming triathlon was going to be harder than I first thought it would be.

I got back in my car and was really concerned with how poor my swim was and that it had triggered a panic attack. The swim at the triathlon was less than three weeks away and it was double the distance. The triathlon also included a run that was double the distance of the one that I had just completed plus a 30-mile bike ride with lots of hills. On my drive home, the only thing I could think to do to get ready for the triathlon was to sign for the stroke and stride the following week and try again. The next week, my swim was a little better; I managed to swim the 1500 meters this time and passed two people on the run. On my car ride home from the second stroke and stride, I decided to sign up again for the next week. I raced again and I got a little bit better. I now was only three days away from my main goal, the triathlon.

The night before the triathlon, torrential rains started falling and continued the morning of the race. The forecast was 60 degrees, but the temperature never rose that high. It may have been late June, but it was 46 degrees and pouring rain. I only had one chance to race before the first anniversary of the accident. I looked up to the sky and smiled and said, "Did you really need to add the torrential rain and freezing temperatures to the race?" I had just gone through the storm of my life, living through my crash, and now I had to race through a literal storm. Sometimes God has a sense of humor. The weather really didn't faze me; if I had to race through a storm, then that is what I was going to do. I was there for the race and a race is what I was going to do.

We plunged into the 59-degree water, and I swam about 100 yards from shore after the starting gun went off. I was having another panic attack; my heart rate was over 200 beats per minute and I was hyperventilating. I was choking on mucus draining from my sinuses. I stopped for a few seconds to calm down and take a bunch of deep breaths. I was really cold and my body was shivering. I knew I just needed to relax, just like I did in the hospital when I had a panic attack. I convinced myself I was okay. I had been through it before. If I had survived it before I could survive it again. I turned back over and started swimming again. The further I swam, the more comfortable and relaxed I became. I started to swim smoothly and started enjoying the swim. I finally reached the shore and exited the water into the 46-degree air. I looked at my watch as I was approaching my bike. I thought my swim had been really slow, especially with the poor start. To my surprise, I swam faster than I had a few days before at the stroke and stride. I was starting to feel more confident.

I got to my bike to change into my biking gear. I started to feel how cold it was. Forty-six degrees is not especially cold, but when you are wet from head to toe and then hop on a bike in the pouring rain, it is quite cold. I was riding carefully as I did not want to crash and break anything that was finally healing. The downpour continued throughout the bike portion of the event. About halfway through the bike ride, I lost feeling in my feet. My feet were soaked and every time I pedaled the water sprayed from my tires all over my feet; my entire body was wet. I had gloves on my hands, but the rain had soaked through them; I had lost all feeling in my hands. I just put my head down and kept pedaling. I knew the only way to get through the bike portion of the race was to ignore my hands and feet and just keep pedaling. More and more people started passing me. My swim wasn't that bad but, on the bike, my injuries from the crash were showing. I just couldn't go fast, no matter how much I tried. I could only pedal one speed, and that was slow. After riding up many hills, I would go down the descents relatively quickly and all I could think the whole time was, *Do not crash*. I didn't want to end up in the hospital again. The rain continued to pour, and it made those fast descents very stressful. In the last third of the bike ride, my gears started to malfunction. The chain started to skip between gears, which made it difficult to pedal. I finally found one gear that was functioning without the chain skipping. Unfortunately, the only gear that worked was a large gear which made it very difficult on my already weary legs to pedal. I finally finished the bike portion and changed into my running shoes. As I changed, I decided my goal was to do the entire run without walking any of it. I started running and my feet and hands were still completely numb. I feared I was going to trip as I ran because I couldn't feel my feet touching the ground and my balance was still not back to normal. About four miles into the 6.2 mile run, I finally got feeling back in my feet and hands. It felt like the run took forever but I finally crossed the finish line and I had managed to run the entire distance. Surprisingly, I did not come in last place. I headed over to the area where they had food for the racers; all that was left were scraps. Now I knew what happened when you finish as slowly as I did.

I packed up my bike and my other gear into my car. I headed home and initially, all I could think about was how many people had passed me during the race. I really had a long way to go if I was ever going to get back to the speed I had been able to go before the crash. I started making a game plan for my future training to get faster. A few minutes later, I stopped thinking about training for a moment and reflected. I was comparing this race to my last memory of this race seven years prior. It wasn't a fair comparison. I hadn't been able to run more than 30 seconds just three months earlier, I couldn't even walk nine months earlier and I had barely made it off that grassy field a year earlier. I had to admit to myself that the race I just completed was quite amazing, considering all the obstacles that I had to overcome just to show up and take this race on. I thought about all the people who had helped me after my crash and during the recovery. The race was partially for me as I had needed a goal to shoot for as I went through over a thousand hours of rehab to get to race day. The race was also for all the people who had helped me along my road to recovery. Often, during recovery, I was asked how I was doing. I could say that I was doing well and summarize my improvements, but it was hard to quantify improvement. There was no measuring stick or exact measurement of how I was doing. This race had been my measuring stick. I could say that I swam 1500 meters, biked 30 miles and ran 6.2 miles during the race. So now, when people asked me how I was doing, I could tell them I completed a race of this distance, and they could use that as a measuring stick for my improvement. It was also a way to finish the story for those medical professionals who had helped me. Now they knew what was possible with their help. They now knew, with certainty, how much they had contributed to my life. Hopefully, whenever they were having a difficult day and they questioned if they were really making a difference, they would remember my story and realize what is possible with all their contributions to patients' lives. They now had the complete story of what happened; from me barely making it to the hospital alive, to the eight day coma, to not being able to put any weight on my legs for three months, to learning to walk again, to running again to finally completing a triathlon in less than a year. Hopefully, they could share the story with other patients going through a difficult time and an uphill battle towards recovery. Those patients could now have the knowledge that if the person in the story could recover, they could too. They could even share the story with other colleagues who were having trouble seeing how important they were to patients; they could tell that person the story that they had witnessed and been a part of.

I got home and took a much-needed nap; that race had wiped me out. I got up from my nap a few hours later, got into my car and headed for the mountains in the western part of Colorado. I had desperately missed looking at those mountains in those three and a half months in the hospital. I decided to take a few days and just take a long drive looking at the mountains to reflect on the past year. I camped that night and woke up the next day. This was the one-year anniversary of the crash. One year ago, today, I had almost died. I replayed the day of the crash as it happened. I thought of the early morning trail run, the sun's reflection off the Flatirons and the breakfast sandwich I had before leaving for the airport. I thought about the jumps I did that day, before the jump where I crashed. I thought of how I felt when I was coming down for a landing when the wind gust hit me from behind and realizing that I may not land on the grass and that there was a distinct possibility that I was going to hit the fence and the building.

Between replaying the events of that day and everything that occurred up until the crash, I thought of all the people who had touched my life during the past year. Without those amazing people, I would not have lived and would not have recovered. Those people chose to help me and chose to invest their time and care in me. On multiple occasions, my therapists would come in and say they had to open their books from therapy school to figure out how to treat my multiple injuries as having all these injured body parts at once made treating me incredibly difficult and challenging. I felt so grateful they were willing to spend their personal time to try to determine how to best help me. I was grateful to be alive; I am truly blessed and everything I went through had a reason for happening. It was up to me to determine what I would get out of this experience. I would have never met so many amazing people, spent three and a half months with my parents and seen my brothers and sister all in such a short period of time. I would never have learned to use my talents, reset my life and get a different perspective on what I was missing and how I should live going forward without this crash.

As the day progressed, I tried to imagine the events that occurred after the crash that I was not aware of; the chaos of when I entered the emergency room to assess what was wrong with me, the determination that the Flight for Life needed to be called, the paramedics loading me into the helicopter trying not to move my body any more than necessary as any movement of my body could have disconnected my heart and killed me instantly. As the sun set, I thought about what my heart surgeon, who just happened to be on call on that Saturday, must have been thinking when he got a call to report to the hospital immediately for an incoming patient who needed emergency surgery. When he woke up that morning did he have any idea that he was about to perform a surgery that neither he, nor any other doctor in that hospital, had ever performed before? What was he thinking after he sawed my sternum open and looked at the challenge he was faced with? A surgery he would later say was one that he remembered how to perform from the textbooks he studied in medical school but had never had the opportunity to perform up until that day as no patient had made it into the hospital alive with the heart injury that I had. As the night and the surgery progressed, did my surgeon question what the chances were that I was going to live? Did he ever wonder what was going on in my mind? Did he ever wonder if I was fighting to survive? Did he ever wonder who he was saving? Did he ever wonder what this person was going to do with his second chance at life, if he could save me?

CHAPTER 19

# Redefining Purpose

Luke 12:48 *"From everyone who has been given much, much will be demanded; and from the one who has been entrusted with much, much more will be asked."*

The finish line of that race was just an arbitrary line drawn on the ground by the race director which signified when they stopped counting the hours, minutes and seconds it took to cover the race distance. That finish line was the fulfillment of a goal that I had set for myself shortly after waking up from the coma; but life moved on. There were other goals. I had other things to accomplish. Rehabilitation didn't stop just because I wasn't going to a rehab facility any longer; it didn't stop because I was not back to where I wanted to be. Since I had gotten out of the hospital, I had a saying that "Everything was rehab." That meant anything, from food shopping, to cleaning the house, to helping a friend move from one house to another was an opportunity to improve and heal. I continued to ride my bike, run, swim and lift weights as I continued to claw my way back to what I had been able to do before the crash. I had no idea if it was possible or not, but I knew the only way that I would find out is if I put all my energy into rehab over a long period of time. There were no quick fixes or fast bounce backs, there was just constant repetition of the same workouts, over and over again, hoping the work would eventually pay off.

As time went on, life started to return to normal. Some days I missed the struggle of the hospital and the time I spent at home rehabbing my injuries. I soon realized that my greatest talents were also my greatest weaknesses. Being single-mindedly focused was amazing for helping me to recover so quickly as it was all I thought about; all I did was rehabilitation. But that single minded, obsessive behavior was also the reason I had been able to work 12-14 hours a day for years on end before the crash. It was the reason I regretted so many things I missed out on prior to the crash.

I realized that, in the real world, all those things I learned weren't as easy to apply as I thought they would be. It is a constant battle to stay focused on the things I wanted to accomplish and things I regretted when I first woke up. When there are so many different distractions and tasks pulling me in different directions, it is challenging to make sure I keep my eye on the important things in life; the things that I want to accomplish. It is my responsibility to figure out how to balance life and not let it overwhelm me and my refocused priorities. After all, I am the one who would regret not changing my life. I would be the one who feels the pain and regret if I don't change. It is not easy, and I can't stand here and tell you I have always won the fight; it is an ongoing battle. I can, however, always look back and reflect on how I felt after waking up from the coma and refocus myself on what is important.

When I was in the rehabilitation hospital, I met many other patients in the cafeteria and observed others in the rehab gym. Many of them were sad and depressed with their situations. Some of them seemed to be in shock or zoned out. During my time in all the hospitals I was in, I realized that mental health support was very limited, at best, and non-existent at worst. I realized from my journey, that fixing my mind was more important than fixing my body. When I fixed my mind, my body followed. I had constant support from my family and some of these people didn't have the same level of support that I did. I tried to help people when I could by listening to their stories in the cafeteria. I tried to lend support and give them encouragement. I was concerned about those patients and have always wondered how everything turned out for them once they left the hospital. Unfortunately, I was not that hopeful as I could see the depression in their eyes and the hopelessness they expressed. After I was discharged, I continued to think about those people.

One of the things that had been on my to do list for years before the crash, was to volunteer at a hospital. I was not sure what I was going to do when I volunteered, but after the crash I felt like I had something I could contribute that most people could not. I now understood what people go through after a life altering accident and the stages of recovery that people experience, mentally and physically. I knew the desperate need for mental health support as it was woefully lacking. I could talk to people who were in recovery, listen to them, give them an encouraging word and offer some direction in their recovery. I could give all of that from the perspective of someone who has gone through it and understands what they are encountering.

I started calling rehab hospitals to volunteer. I left voicemail after voicemail after voicemail with none of them being returned. I thought volunteering and helping others was supposed to be the easy part of this journey. I was frustrated and discouraged. I thought this was supposed to be my calling. This was one of the reasons I was given a second chance. Wasn't it? I was eager to help; I felt like I could make a meaningful contribution in the lives of people going through some of the toughest events they have ever faced.

Wasn't this supposed to be part of God's plan for me? Then, Covid hit and there was no chance a rehab hospital was going to allow anyone to volunteer. I felt like I was doing nothing to help others. As frustration built up, something unexpected happened that helped me change my perception of how I was supposed to be helping people. I didn't have to search for people who needed my help. I didn't need to be in a hospital to help people. Suddenly, people I knew personally started going through difficult times and needed help. My Mom broke her leg, my coworker broke her ankle, a friend had his gall bladder removed, a friend had to go through surgery to remove cancer, my niece broke her arm, my Dad had a cancerous brain tumor removed, I had another surgery that I had to deal with, another person I know had surgery on their intestine, a friend had hernia surgery, another friend was battling eye problems and surgery and another coworker had cancer surgery and I got to visit him in the hospital. Sometimes, I just listened to them voice their concerns and fears, talk about their experiences in the hospital or talk about their prognosis as they felt comfortable talking to someone who had had similar experiences. Other times, I would tell them how to best deal with the insurance company or what they could expect from physical therapy. As they talked to me, I could identify what stage of recovery they were in and I tried to talk to them based on that stage to help them to get to the next stage of recovery.

Helping people I knew allowed me to finally use some of the lessons that I learned during my recovery. It felt like I was finally doing what I was meant to do with my second chance; but without having a place to volunteer I could only help people I knew. Until the hospitals opened and allowed volunteers again, I felt like I was wasting time. There had to be something else that I could do. While helping people who were in immediate need was one way to help people, how else could I reach people who weren't in hospitals? Maybe they hadn't gone through that difficult trial in their life yet, or they were going through that difficult time in their life but were no longer in a hospital; perhaps what they were going through did not require them to be in a hospital. Would sharing my story help those people as well?

I thought back to a time, earlier in my life, when I had been asked to give a sermon in my church as a senior in high school. After that first sermon, every summer while I was in college, the minister asked a few of the college kids to do a sermon while we were home from school. A few years after giving one of those sermons, my youngest brother, who was nine when I had given the sermon, quoted the Bible verse that I talked about. I was taken aback that he remembered it years later. If he remembered that sermon, years later, maybe someone else did. Maybe speaking in front of people was a talent that I had not been taking advantage of. Maybe I finally had a message that needed to be shared that could help others.

I had been thinking about those lessons I had learned in the hospital and during rehab every time I had been out on a walk or hike since the crash. I now had to finally sit down and recount my story in a notebook with the goal of crafting that story into a thirty minute sermon to share with others. Over the next few weeks, I wrote down everything I could remember from the experience. I would finish every session mentally exhausted. I was reliving all those dark days that I had been through; reliving all those regrets and emotions that I dealt with when I woke up from that coma and all the pain I had endured in the hospital. Living through the experience again, in all that detail, was what I had to do if I was going to be able to recount my story and share it with others and hopefully help them with the trials they would face or were currently facing. If I wasn't willing to confront everything that I went through again, how was I going to help others?

After writing everything down about the experience that I could remember, I started to craft the experience into a sermon. I continued to write and rewrite and rewrite the sermon again and again. I finally got to a point where I was willing to share the sermon with a friend. I had shared parts of my story many times previously but now, sharing all of it at once, I was really putting myself out there. It was extremely personal. I am a private person and not someone who shares their emotions often. It was a nerve-racking experience just allowing my friend to read it. I questioned whether I was ready to share such a deeply personal experience with people I didn't know if it was already this difficult to allow my friend to read it.

After my friend read it, she encouraged me that this was something I should share; that the words I had written were powerful and could help others. In my time of doubt, it was the encouragement that I needed. After spending so much time writing in isolation, I had started doubting whether I had a message to share with people or whether I was fooling myself. After getting feedback from my friend, I knew my self-doubt was my fear of putting myself out there, not the fear that I didn't have a message that was worth sharing. Fear is there to protect you, but it can also hold you back from doing things that make you uncomfortable. I had to decide what type of fear this was. I knew sharing my story was not something I *should* do, it was something that I *had to* do. If I didn't share it to help others, then I was wasting my second chance at life. I was here for a reason. Now that I had the speech completed, I needed to find a place that would allow me to speak. I wasn't a well-known public figure. No one was looking for me to speak. If I wanted to speak, I had to be the one to help convince someone to allow me to speak in front of their congregation. Luckily, the friend who read my speech was also an ordained minister. She wasn't working in a church at the time, but she put me in touch with another minister to check if they would be interested. After a few phone calls over a few months with the minister and my friend recommending me as a speaker, he agreed to let me speak.

Over the weeks leading up to speaking, I continued to revise my speech and practice over and over. I felt a great sense of responsibility; if that minister was willing to allow me to speak to his congregation, I needed to provide a message that would be helpful. The fear and anxiety started to build. Could I speak on such a deeply personal experience and convey my message?

The day finally came for me to speak. I woke up hours too early as I had an abundance of nervous energy. I had so many extra hours before I needed to leave the house that I practiced the speech a few more times and went for a walk to watch the sunrise. I then got dressed and got into my car and headed to the church. As I drove to the church, the drive brought me south of town. It was the same drive I had taken on the day of the crash, when I went for a trail run before I went skydiving. The sun illuminated the Flatirons, just like it had the morning of the crash. I proceeded to drive south, and I drove right past the orthopedic office of the three doctors who had performed multiple surgeries on me; this was also the office where I had completed eight months of outpatient physical therapy. The drive was like going down memory lane. I proceeded south and turned off the main road to head to the church. I hadn't realized the church was located two blocks from the hospital I had arrived at via the Flight for Life helicopter. I decided to turn into the hospital's parking lot. I sat in the parking lot and thought about everything that had happened in that hospital. I was overwhelmed with emotion just by seeing the hospital. I had no idea that I would be affected so much by the sight of the hospital. I was reliving everything I was about to share with the church in my sermon. I started my car again and drove around the hospital, just as I always did when I passed by. On the drive around the hospital, I saw the Flight For Life helicopter sitting there on the pad, waiting for its next call. I finished circling the hospital and then drove the two blocks to the church. I was the first person in the parking lot and I was an emotional mess. I questioned if I could really deliver the sermon that day. Just like there was a reason why I had been in that crash, there must be a reason that the first church I gave a sermon in required me to drive past so many of the places that were a part of my story.

As the time to speak approached, I started to channel the emotion from that morning. I said a little prayer, asking God to give me the strength to preach His message. I got up and started speaking. I had this negative self-talk in the back of my mind during the first 30 seconds of my sermon; that made me question if I could get through it. I took a deep breath and kept going and that doubt dissipated after a few minutes. Speaking was not that much different than skydiving. Once I jumped out of the plane there was no going back in, things may go wrong at some point, and I had to fix whatever that was based on the practice I had done previously. I was completely in the moment during that sermon. Those 45 minutes felt like five minutes. I finished the sermon, sat down and just hoped that I had helped at least one person that day.

The service ended and people from the congregation started to come up to me; they thanked me for sharing my story. Then someone came up to me and started sharing their story about an accident they had been in and how it changed their life and how me speaking that day helped them remember the struggle they had been through. It felt amazing to connect to another person who had gone through a similar experience. Someone else came up to me and said that whenever they go through the next trial in their life, they will remember my story and use it to help make it through. It felt amazing, like I had found my calling.

I went home and reached out to more than 20 churches to try to set up more speaking engagements. Unfortunately, I found out that churches weren't as welcoming as I thought they would be. Most of my emails asking ministers to meet with me to discuss opportunities to speak at their churches were not responded to. The only one that was returned questioned whether I was legitimate or whether my true motivation was to network with their congregation to sell them financial products. My temporary excitement that I had finally found my calling was quickly brought back to reality. If this was why I was given a second chance, why was it so difficult? It took a few weeks to realize this must be part of God's plan for me and I had to be patient. Just as I thought I needed to be in a hospital to help people going through trials in their lives, maybe I wasn't recognizing all the opportunities that may be available to share the message.

I continued to follow up with the churches I had reached out to with no success when finally, my friend who had helped me with my first speaking engagement called and asked if I would speak at a new church that she had become the minister of. It was the lifeline I needed. I spoke again. To my amazement, people from the congregation asked me if I would like to be connected to other people they knew to speak to other groups. Their kindness was amazing and gave me hope again that I could speak to more people and that people thought my message was valuable enough that more people needed to hear it. One of the church members came over to me after the service to let me know that one of her close friends had been in a rehab hospital for many months and was feeling down. She inquired if I would be willing to talk to him. I found out that the hospital where he was staying was only thirty minutes from the church where I had just spoken and I headed there after the service. If I hadn't been at the church speaking that day, I would never have had the opportunity to speak to this person who was struggling in the hospital. Nothing that happened that day was by accident; it was part of the plan. I visited the hospital and sat there and listened. He expressed a lot of feelings similar to what I had gone through while I was in rehab. Most importantly, he talked about what he wanted to do once he got out of rehab which told me he was looking forward to getting out even though he had a few weeks before he was scheduled to be discharged. The fact that he had plans for the future made me smile when I left the hospital because I knew it meant that he was in a good place and would be ready to resume his life when he got out.

That speaking engagement led to another one two weeks later. I finished the speech and had an amazing question and answer session with the congregation. At the end of the Q & A, a member of the congregation told me a story of a friend of his who was going through a really difficult time in her life and he feared that her problems with addiction were leading her down a path that was going to end badly. I asked if it would help if I went to visit her and he said she was not going to answer her phone or door for anyone. He then asked if I had any recordings of my sermon as he thought it may help her if she heard it. I explained it was only my third time giving my sermon and I only had a rough recording from two weeks prior that I could give him a link to. On my drive home, his request made me think. No matter how many times I share my story, I may not be reaching all the people that may benefit from hearing it. Maybe the lesson I needed to learn by getting no responses from churches and rehab hospitals was to change my perception of how I could share my story and help others. Friends and family had suggested I write a book once I got out of the hospital and at the time I hadn't really considered it. I am not a writer and who was going to read a book that I wrote? That day, it became clear that no one can read a book that has not been written. If writing a book was another way of reaching the people that I couldn't help by visiting a hospital, or meeting face to face, then I had to write one. As I learned from the crash and rehab, God has a plan for me. I'm not always sure what the plan is, but my life would not be what it is today, and have a redefined purpose, if I hadn't jumped for the third time that day.

CHAPTER 20

# Miracles

**Luke 1:37** *"For nothing is impossible with God."*

A week after coming home from the hospital, I walked over to the manager's office of the housing complex that I lived in. I wanted to thank the manager for helping prepare my bathroom before I came home from the hospital. They had installed a removable shower head that allowed me to hold it in my hand so I could use it while sitting on a bench that was installed in my shower. They also added railings in my bathroom to help me get around, keep me safe and prevent me from falling. When I opened the door to the office, I saw a gentleman who was in his mid 20's. I asked if I could see Karen, the manager. He got the manager; I thanked her for all her help and she gave me a hug. We talked about the crash and my experience at the hospital for a few minutes and she said she was so happy I was home. She went back into her office and the young gentleman sat down at his desk. As I turned around to head for the door he said, "Now that you have lived through the crash, everything from now on should be easy." I stopped and turned around and replied, "Just because I made it through one trial doesn't mean there isn't another one about to begin. One trial just prepares you for the next." I'm not sure that was the answer he was expecting and then he quickly asked, "What is the secret to life?" I looked at him and said, "Build a strong foundation. I got through my toughest days by applying lessons I learned over my lifetime. All those lessons I had previously learned guided me. All those lessons came back to me when I needed them. It's a roadmap for getting through your trials." He stared at me with a blank look. I suppose it wasn't the easy shortcut he was looking for.

I had, unknowingly, been preparing for this trial for my entire life. God had a plan for me, and that plan prepared me with everything I needed to know in order to get through this trial. Every time I wasn't sure what direction to turn in or what to do, a lesson from the past came to me and I was able to apply it; whether it was understanding that going through trials tests your faith and develops perseverance or that God will not let you be tempted beyond what you can bear and will provide a way out. When you are weary and burdened, he will give you rest. Having faith without taking action is useless. A lot will be expected of a person when a lot is given to them. Be who you proclaim that you have been all along, even when times are toughest; if you have dug deep and laid your foundation on rock, your house will not be shaken when the flood comes.

The scripture, and miracles in the Bible, aren't just things that happened a long time ago. The scriptures are just as relevant today as they were when written, you just need to apply them. Miracles happen today just as they happened thousands of years ago; I wouldn't be alive today without a miracle having occurred. The doctor that saved my life told my family that no doctor in that hospital had ever performed the surgery he performed on my heart on any patient previously because no one had ever made it to the hospital alive with the injury that I had. He said he only knew how to perform the surgery because he remembered how to do it from his medical school textbook. The day after the surgery he stood in my room, staring at me, until my friend, who was the first to arrive at the hospital after my surgery, asked in a concerned manner why was he staring at me for such a long time and if something was wrong. The doctor replied, "I can't believe he is alive! He should have never made it off the field alive, never made it to the hospital alive or made it through surgery alive. No one survives what he just survived!"

I'm just a normal person, not any different from anyone else. I was blessed to have God intercede in my life at a moment when I needed Him most. He listened when I needed Him to listen, He watched over me when I asked Him to and He gave me what I needed, when I needed it.

God has wisdom beyond what we can comprehend sometimes and has a plan for all of us. It doesn't mean that it is going to be easy, or without pain; but He is not looking to harm us. He is looking to give us hope and a future.

Every day, I am reminded of what happened as every time I get dressed I see the scar that goes from my upper chest all the way down to my belt line. It is the scar I never want to go away, it's a reminder every day to think about what my life was, how I got off track and that God saved me for a reason and gave me a purpose in life again.

# About the Author

Jason Dennen is a Christian, author, inspirational speaker, skydiver, mountain climber, triathlete, and explorer. He was born and raised in New Jersey. He moved to Colorado to explore the wide-open spaces in the west and test his limits. He currently lives in Boulder, Colorado. Jason can be contacted at JasonDennentheHealer@gmail.com

Jason is on a mission to inspire people by sharing his story of survival and to empower people to get through life's most difficult hardships by utilizing the lessons they have already learned throughout their lives and by taking advantage of the strength, they already possess inside themselves.

# NOTES

# NOTES

# NOTES

# NOTES

# NOTES

# NOTES

Printed in the USA
CPSIA information can be obtained
at www.ICGtesting.com
LVHW022352050224
770993LV00001B/316

9 798986 147376